Corporate
Communication
for Managers

Corporate Communication for Managers

Peter C. Jackson

PITMAN PUBLISHING
128 Long Acre, London WC2E 9AN

©Longman Group UK Ltd 1987

First published in Great Britain 1987

British Library Cataloguing in Publication Data
Jackson, Peter C
  Corporate communication for managers
  1. Communication in management
  2. Communication in organizations
  I. Title
  658.4'5   HD30.3

ISBN 0 273 02688 7

Typeset by Avocet Marketing Services, Bicester, Oxon.
Printed and bound in Great Britain at
the Bath Press, Avon

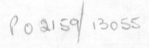

Contents

Acknowledgements

My thanks to the following publications, associations, companies, individuals and publishers for quotations and case histories used in this book and for helpful advice.

The editors of *Business, Capital Magazine, Fortune, Industrial Society, The Listener, PR Week, The Sunday Times*; The Investor Relations Society; The International Association of Business Communicators; The Institute of Public Relations for 'Sword of Excellence' case studies; British Telecom; The Burton Group plc; Cadbury Schweppes plc; Chemical Industries Association Ltd; Digital Equipment Corp; IBM UK Ltd; National Westminster Bank plc; Paragon Communications plc; Strathclyde Regional Council; Touche Ross & Co; Towers, Perrin, Forster & Crosby Inc; Trusthouse Forte plc; Valin Pollen International; Arthur Young & Co; Don Craib; Sir Nicholas Goodison; Sir Peter Parker; Eric Silvester; Nigel Rowe; Norman Woodhouse. HM Stationery Office for extracts from *The Complete Plain Words* by Sir Ernest Gowers; Penguin Books Ltd for extracts from *The Winning Streak* by Walter Goldsmith and David Clutterbuck.

My special thanks to William Beaver, Director of Publicity, Dr Barnardo's, who encouraged me to write this book and has been a valuable and persuasive influence in its completion.

Also available from Pitman
A Communication Audit Handbook
S C Hamilton

1
Clearing a path

Corporate Communication rules OK?

OF COURSE COMPANIES should communicate – and not just for the sake of communication! Using the means without holding clearly defined objectives leads only to frustration and disappointment. There must be something to communicate *about*. There must be someone to communicate *with*.

But for too long company communication has been seen as an optional extra; a gimmick bundled in with the corporate cornflakes to be seized upon or discarded depending on the appetites of the Board and the mood of the Chief Executive.

Communication is more than this: it is the means by which any company, every company, from the self-sufficient multi-national to the three-men-and-a-word-processor new business, continues to trade and make a profit. It is the way in which the company makes and keeps contact with those who affect its life and growth: salesmen and supervisors, dealers and analysts, bankers and customers, investors and politicians.

Much is said today about 'company image' and 'company culture'. These are simply the outward face and the inward spirit of any group of people working together, and both image and culture are enhanced by effective corporate communication.

But what exactly *is* corporate communication?

Some might suggest it is a service provided by an advertising agency or public relations consultancy to develop better company relations with Government and the City. Others have said that it is about

'Helping to shape an organisation's response to the problems it faces in a critical world and suggesting actions which demonstrate that it

3

cares not only about its own people, but the community – and the world – at large.'

Corporate communication might also be confused with a corporate identity campaign, involving designers and copywriters, or perhaps the ways in which corporate issues are managed or corporate crises resolved.

So far as this book is concerned, corporate communication is none and all of these things. It is

THE TOTAL COMMUNICATION ACTIVITY GENERATED BY A COMPANY TO ACHIEVE ITS PLANNED OBJECTIVES

It is the company – or the corporation if you prefer – communicating to whichever audiences and with whatever media it cares to choose, *providing* it is aiming to achieve selected and planned objectives.

Advertising and public relations and corporate design are thus *part* of corporate communication – and not the other way round! This may be an unconventional approach (and unacceptable to some practitioners) but it makes sense. And, more importantly, it brings corporate communication out of the swamp of consultancy jargon and plants it firmly within the daily working experience of every company manager.

The wood for the trees

The trouble with corporate communication is that most of us think we're rather good at it. The ever-expanding graveyard of failed presentations, aborted brochures, incoherent speeches, discarded press releases and splintered images suggests otherwise.

Why is this? Could it be that most company managers share that view of communication as an optional extra; something which can be attended to *after* the next sale has been closed or the production run finished or the agreement negotiated? Could it be that most company managers think of communication as always being someone else's responsibility – the marketing director or the chairman or that public relations firm we took on last year? Could it be that most company managers are reluctant to get involved with communication because it was never part of their training and they are hesitant over its terminology and suspicious of its claims?

Surely these are *all* part of the problem: the reluctance to give communication its proper place at the cutting edge of corporate life; the belief that communication is a distant function performed by specialists; the lack of training in communication appreciation and techniques.

All those individual thickets of communication activity – the annual report, the employee briefing group, the advertising campaign, the dealers' newspaper, the press launch, the speakers' panel – grow into a jungle of specialisms. The company manager either tires of trying to understand this communication barrier and walks the long way round or attempts to break through the undergrowth, only to be sidetracked by inexperience, ambushed by experts, and bound and gagged by apathy and non-delegation.

This book tries to provide a way through that wood. It is not a guide for the specialists; they have been here before and many of the trees are hatched with their initials. Neither does it provide a step-by-step route for the whole terrain; every manager has different needs and each company differing requirements.

The main purpose of this guidebook is to try to see the wood *in spite of* the trees, for communication blunders in business and industry so often stem from the failure to view the operation as an entire programme, not a series of unrelated events and objects. The aim is to enable the company manager to appreciate the value of an *integrated* corporate communication programme.

Audiences, messages, media

Let's begin by clearing a path to see what lies ahead.

First we'll look at the Company itself: what it's made of and how it reacts to competition, change and crisis.

Then the Communicators within the company:

▷ **The Chief Executive and the Board who must provide commitment to communication while recognising the need for delegation to their managers.**
▷ **The senior and middle management who must be prepared to carry through communication policies, both internally and externally.**

Next, the Audiences, both inside and out:

▷ *Employee-related* such as office and factory staff, junior managers and supervisors, trade unionists and graduates, pensioners and prospective employees.

▷ *Product-related* such as customers and distributors, suppliers and franchise holders, dealers and the general public, action groups and educators.

▷ *Finance-related*, including small and institutional investors, brokers' analysts, banks and Government departments.

▷ *Government-related* such as local and county councils, MPs, civil servants and local interest groups.

We'll also need to consider the Messages, those facts and figures and expressions of belief and values which the company has to communicate because:

▷ They have been *legislated* by forces outside company control.

▷ They are facts which company audiences *want to know*.

▷ They are facts which the company *wants to communicate*.

Having scanned the messages, we will discuss how they need

to be transmitted by a selection of the Media including:

▷ *Face-to-face* interviews, talks, briefing groups, speeches, discussions and meetings of all kinds.
▷ *Marks on paper* including advertisements, newsletters, bulletins and magazines, newspapers and leaflets, brochures and books.
▷ *Sound and vision* which includes electric and electronic media such as film, slide, video and audio and also the use of sponsorship.

We will then meet the Specialists, both within and outside the company, who have a vital role in helping to identify the audiences, select and refine the messages and effectively use the media.

After examining how these ingredients can be mixed together to achieve specific objectives, we conclude by considering the value of Research within a planned communication strategy.

If only we could communicate

Such a plan is not particularly original. To consider the senders and the receivers, the messages themselves and the means by which they can be sent is elementary communication theory. Yet isn't that part of the problem? Hasn't the business of communicating within and outside the company become so overgrown with specialist jargon, so choked with KEEP OFF notices and PRIVATE PROPERTY warnings that many of us have forgotten the first objective?

> '*Everything will be all right if only we could communicate,*' Jan Masaryk said, '*but the trouble is – we seldom do.*'

By exploring the corporate communication jungle in this way you, as a manager – whatever your level, however wide or narrow your responsibilities – will bring the possibility of effective corporate communication one step closer.

Effective corporate communication is not something to be left only to specialists, nor is it an optional extra on the management timetable: it should be an essential, integral part of every manager's working life. So grasp whatever guidance you can from the pages that follow and, if you want everything to have the best chance of being all right in your own department or division or company,

ONLY COMMUNICATE

We take the first steps in this exploration of the communication jungle by looking around us: at the collection of human, financial and practical resources which make up the organisation for which we work, whether manufacturing, business or service industry.

The Company – what is it and why does it need communication?

2
Companies under pressure

The harsh light of competition

WHEN THE BIG BANG exploded on 27 October 1986 it jolted every pin-striped leg in the City of London.

As Bang Day approached, major City institutions engaged in a frenzy of takeovers, mergers and alliances. Sudden wealth showered into the pockets of head-hunters, financial consultants, public relations companies and advertising agencies. Teams of computer-literate executives were hawked from one firm to the next with all the expense and razzamatazz of a bunch of star football players.

Why all this activity? Because many companies, stripped of the traditional wrappings which had insulated them against bruising reality, were being exposed to the harsh light of competition for the first time. They were struggling to survive – not merely from the onslaughts of other British financial firms but from the predatory claws of the newly-admitted Americans and Japanese.

Such exposure has a salutary effect. It sends managements running: some for cover, pulling skimpy contingency plans around their ears; others in ever-decreasing circles; others in search of 'expert' help. As one partner in a leading stockbroking firm told *Capital Magazine* post-Bang:

'My bloody office now looks like mission control centre for one of those space shows. There was a time when you knew your clients personally: their wives, names of their kids, that sort of thing. Now I have to deal with names like TALISMAN, SEAQ and SEPON, all faceless electronic gadgets I can't for the life of me fully understand.'

13

THIS MANAGERIAL WITHDRAWAL from the brink of change is not limited to stockbrokers. Your own company has to face and accept change and it can best do so by *using* change to help improve efficiency and expand its sphere of operation. And this demands effective corporate communication.

The activity-provoking beam projected by the City of London's Big Bang was not a new phenomenon for industry and commerce. Wall Street had its own Big Bang in 1975 when fixed brokerage commissions were abolished, leading to a price war. In the United Kingdom the lifting of restrictions on selling spectacles, mortgages and, immediately after the Second World War, petrol and soft drinks, produced similar flurries of competition. Those who communicated were the winners.

Take Schweppes, who during Wartime rationing had to produce beverages and squashes under the common Soft Drinks Industry label sponsored by the Ministry of Food. They had no branded products but that didn't stop them communicating and they launched an inventive series of press advertisements looking forward to the products' return. In the words of one nostalgic ad:

> *'If we had some gin we'd have a gin and tonic if we had some Schweppes.'*

This determination to communicate not only kept the name alive in the public mind but led to the launch of the first great Schweppes advertising campaign with its memorable catchword 'Schweppervescence'.

Never the same again

At times of crisis and competition it's easy to prophesy 'Things will never be the same again!' Another senior partner battling with faceless electronic gadgets said:

> '*Stockbroking's not fun any more. And it used to be, marvellous it was. But if I was starting out now I wouldn't go near this business.*'

The results of change are rarely as catastrophic as the prediction. It *will* be fun and many others *will* go into the business. But, equally, there will be unfamiliar coats on the hallstand and new faces in the dining room. Things will never *quite* be as they once were and, more importantly, a lesson has been learned; it is that

COMPETITION MEANS COMMUNICATION

Communication is essential if your company is to survive. How many times have managements, facing a possible strike, a drop in sales, or high employee turnover, echoed Jan Masaryk's words: 'Everything will be all right if only we could communicate'?

How many times have *you* said it, facing bad feeling in your department, a lack of understanding by others of your own problems, a breakdown in relationships?

'Everything will be all right – if only I could make contact – if only I could get them to understand – if only I could explain – if only I could communicate.

The trouble is we seldom do, and when we don't it's so easy

to blame failure on the department or the division or the company itself.

'Our communication system failed again', we say, as if communication was something like the National Grid, too high and far off for us to influence. Not so: communication is essentially a personal matter and we are all part of the plan.

Surviving in silence

Of course, despite the Golden Rules which embellish this and other management handbooks, it is perfectly possible for a company to exist *without* communicating effectively with its audiences; indeed, some deliberately choose to keep a low profile.

For instance, Cap Gemini Sogeti claimed to be the largest independent professional computer software and service supplier in Europe in 1986, according to *Business*. Yet this company, said the magazine, was virtually unknown among US stockbroking firms and in the UK it was active for five years before it appointed a public relations consultancy. As the general manager of CGS UK explained:

'It's not in our culture to say "Here we are!"'

Similarly, in the City of London there were those who covered their corporate eyes and pretended that the Big Bang would not happen. When, shortly before financial deregulation, stockbrokers Cazenove and Company were asked how they were going to react to the approaching explosion, a senior partner gave a tentative reply:

'Well, you know, we're rather reluctant in coming forward, always.'

What about talking to the Press?

'It's just that we aren't very good at it and always get ourselves in a sort of muddle, you know. Nothing particular to hide; just that we aren't very good at sort of poking our noses over the parapet. It seems increasingly difficult to keep behind the parapet but, you know, I think we're going to try and do so if we can.'

Such deliberate reticence is not to be imitated. As restrictions are lifted, as information becomes more open, as employees, customers and shareholders – let alone the Press – become more inquisitive, so heads *must* show above the parapet. No company can be so insular if it values its profitable existence. Bhopal, Tylenol and Chernobyl have shown that it is less and less possible for an industrial or political monopoly to keep silent in the face of a global demand for information.

When the weekend safety experiment at Chernobyl went so disastrously wrong, it was four months before the first report was submitted by the USSR to the International Atomic Energy Authority – and the expectant millions of the televised world. Ian McDougall concluded in *The Listener* that:

'There were really two disasters at Chernobyl. The first, and obviously biggest, was the threat to human life and health. The second was the response to the disaster by the Soviet information services – a response that can at best be described as tardy and grudging, at worst as unworthy of a great power. It's this second disaster, as recorded by the BBC listening monitors at Caversham, that raises once again the question of Soviet credibility as a whole.'

Smears and rumours

It is just that question of corporate credibility which smears any organisation when there is lack of information and the same tired evasions are brought out like whitewash at times of crisis.

> *'Between you and me old boy, Harrison had let things slip. Not exactly a resignation matter, but now he's gone I'm sure you'll see an improvement in our service.'*

Another familiar sidestep:

> *'Those blessed components failed again I'm afraid. I blame the suppliers. Seems impossible to get decent quality these days.'*

Such shallow excuses have all too often been trailed across the executive blotter or the company letterhead. But – at Chernobyl as in Chelmsford or Chicago – only collective responsibility, freely admitted and promptly communicated, can be the acceptable corporate response to crisis.

Competition, change and crisis all put pressure on the company to communicate more effectively. There is also now a greater amount of floating corporate wealth in the West which is enabling more companies to tread the shadowy corridors of Takeover House and riffle through the sloping shelves. And those companies that have, by choice or negligence, adopted an insular, restrictive, uncommunicative stance, will be the first to slide down to the front of the shelf and feel the constricting grip of an unwelcome buyer.

NO COMPANY IS AN ISLAND

and it has to relate, to communicate, with a wide range of audiences if it is to survive under these pressures.

See, for example, what a company such as IBM has achieved with an almost fanatical dedication to corporate communication. Its Big Blue Brother approach may not be to everyone's liking, but the way it has stuck to a detailed communication programme over many years has brought deserved benefits.

Its corporate communication plan ranges from inspired advertising to imaginative customer interface; from sparkling company reporting to excellent employee information programmes; from the masterly local community activities adopted in the UK in the late 1960s to influential sponsorship on both sides of the Atlantic. It is also one of the major companies which stresses the importance of communication by managers.

Both ends of the spectrum

These are the extremes of the spectrum we are about to view. Not many large companies are as reticent as CGS; few are as wholeheartedly communicative as IBM. Yet it is towards the Big Blue end of the spectrum that we should strive to position our own company.

This company of ours is, after all, no more than a ball of solid facts and hot air, spinning through inter-corporate space. Out there, beyond the circling rings of directors, managers and staff, are the worlds of customers, shareholders and the general public. Further out still are the remote constellations of journalists, analysts, suppliers, graduates and pressure groups. And every once in a while another corporate ball will spin into view and force a file to be opened, labelled either Potential Customers or Takeover Defences.

There is no question of simply *not* relating in this situation, of *not* communicating; for even if it does nothing but spin, your company will be judged, in spite of itself, by its very silence in the corporate galaxy. So why not help it to communicate positively?

Remember, your company is *not* an island and to survive in today's harsh business environment of competition, change and crisis *must* involve planned corporate communication.

Commitment to communication should follow commitment to profit in the company's Ten Commandments. Ten Commandments implies some kind of law-giver and who that is and how he or she relates to the rest of the company communicators is the subject of our next chapter.

3
A communicating management

As good as a wink

AT THE ROOFING felt manufacturers just outside Manchester, a whiff of suppressed excitement mingled with the usual smell of bitumen blowing across from the coating bay. It was visiting day for the Group Chairman; the canteen was bright with unaccustomed flowers and the lino gleamed. Five minutes to go and up on the platform company and local dignitaries were assembling. The Divisional Director took his seat by the Company Managing Director and whispered behind a cupped hand.

'Is someone going to thank the Chairman?'

'Yes. Jenkins will do it. I've arranged that when I give him the nod he'll say "Three cheers for Mr Waters". Just after the old boy's speech I thought.'

'Splendid', said the Divisional Director. And then, 'Which one is Jenkins?'

'Over there in the cap', replied the MD, nodding towards the third row.

Seeing the pre-arranged signal, Jenkins leapt to his feet, took off his cap and said loudly, 'Three cheers for Mr Waters. Hip, hip ...'

As the embarrassed Managing Director looked on in shocked disbelief, sixty-five Mancunians bellowed the customary response.

ON SUCH SMALL ACTS of communication or miscommunication between people in companies is success or disaster finely balanced.

As that incident illustrates, no matter how carefully we prepare a communication programme to achieve our corporate objectives, it is the way people behave within that programme which is the crucial factor. So we must study these people – the communicators – and try to ascertain how they are likely to affect communication, for good or ill, and what their needs and their relationships are. Only then can we begin to structure a communication policy in which they can be effectively involved.

Why kowtow to culture?

Some believe that it is the company itself, not its people, which influences its communication structure. The proponents of 'corporate culture' suggest that over the years any company builds up its own self-regulating mechanism; its own unique amalgam of tradition, habits, cyclical sales patterns, preferences, attitudes, morals, mores, as well as the more tangible manifestations of logos, trademarks and advertising campaigns.

And culture, suggests Richard Pascale in *Fortune*, is inextricably linked with success:

> '*A strong culture – a set of shared values, norms, and beliefs that gets everybody heading in the same direction – is common to all the companies held up as paragons in* In Search of Excellence.'

Such corporate culture not only produces a similar outlook in successive generations of employees (the subject of Pascale's study), but must limit its management to act in a predictable pattern.

If this were really the case it would be pointless to exhort any manager reading this page to change the way the company communicates. What the company *is* would automatically control what it *did*.

In fact, experience shows that when company culture so dominates employees, there may be negative effects as well as positive, when new ideas are stifled and essential change resisted.

> '*It's sad to contemplate how many dedicated employees sincerely want to do a good job and yet feel their corporate cultures working quite effectively in opposition to their efforts.*'

So wrote a disillusioned executive to *Fortune*.

As for a culture-dominated chief executive, more often it is the chief executive and the board who dominate and change the culture. Lord Weinstock of GEC and Serge Kampf of CGS have personally been responsible for their companies' non-communicative bias. On the other hand, Lee Iacocca of Chrysler, John Egan at Jaguar and Sir John Harvey-Jones at ICI are men who have changed the culture rather than allow the culture to change them.

Face at the top

For the employee and the business journalist, the corporate

face is increasingly that of its Top Man (or Woman), be they chief executive, chairman, or managing director. Whether authorising a multi-million pound advertising campaign, or vetting a policy statement in the company newspaper, or speaking to shareholders or analysts on video film, the Top Man is almost always the Almighty Finger which sparks the communication programme into life.

True, there are faceless exceptions. Few could have named the Top Man at ICI before Sir John Harvey-Jones took over. The same is true of Unilever and many of the oil multinationals. But in general, industry has followed politics and crystallised its public face into that of one person.

In the United Kingdom this has been particularly true of the nationalised industries, where any labour dispute or talk of privatisation immediately narrows the perspective onto one man, as it did with Ian MacGregor, Chairman of the National Coal Board (now British Coal) in the bitter months of the miners' strike of 1984–5.

Throughout that dispute the Coal Board's public relations team provided a round-the-clock service to the media, seven days every week, and as part of this service managers throughout the industry were communicating at local level. But for the majority of the onlookers the fight – for fight it was – was between Ian MacGregor and Arthur Scargill, President of the National Union of Mineworkers.

British Coal's Director of Public Relations, Norman Woodhouse, puts the blame for this polarisation on television:

'In times of industrial strife television producers are persistently *seeking to present gladiatorial spectacles of top people in industry and the unions slogging it out in confrontational debate, on the pretence that viewers will be able to weigh up the arguments and decide who to blame or support.'*

In fact, although Ian MacGregor and his negotiators met Arthur Scargill and union officials on no fewer than 20 occasions for 120 hours of talks, the two men had only *one* actual confrontation: for *Channel 4 News* and from separate studios.

However, there is no doubt that for the wider world, brought up on political figurehead confrontations, and for most of those within business and industry, the company *is* the chief executive; and this means that so far as overall responsibility for internal and external communication is concerned, the buck stops right there.

So often, because Top Men do not delegate or communicate themselves, that is where it stays. At management conferences chief executives and chairmen say all the right things: 'Communication programme vital ... must tell employees ... honest and believable interface with the outside world ... blah ... blah'.

The outside world waits, with bated breath. And waits. And nothing happens.

As in so many areas of management life, the theory has to be put into practice and that cannot be done by chief executives alone, no matter how high their enthusiasm. But, make no mistake, their word, their whim, can totally inspire or unhinge the corporate communication programme, corporate culture notwithstanding, and so there must always be

A FIRM COMMITMENT AT THE TOP

Breaking the bottleneck

Once policy has been decided at the top, the actual spadework *must* be handled through the management chain. Law-givers often fail to notice that the messages are stopping one or two tiers below them where managers are *not* communicating because they are uninformed and unenthusiastic.

Uninformed managers lack contacts, information and commitment to company objectives. They are disillusioned. Why? In the UK they have seen salary differentials eroded while still having to take responsibility for getting the job done. They have seen powers of employment and dismissal made more difficult by legislation. They have seen that growth of information for unions and other participative structures has often meant that those working for them know more than they do about what's happening in the company.

One of my jobs for a large UK group was to produce the annual report for employees. It went out, in all its multi-coloured glory, with sparkling prose and all-human-life-is-there pictures. The staff sat back and congratulated themselves. A month later we launched a survey to see how the report had been received.

At one large factory all the employees had ticked the box labelled 'not seen' so we asked some more questions. Investigation revealed that the pack of 500 reports was still sitting behind the telephone shelf in reception because the managers were not concerned enough to arrange for them to be distributed.

Yet it is on these very managers that successful communication depends because

MANAGERS ARE THE KEY TO EFFECTIVE CORPORATE COMMUNICATION

Corporate communication programmes are essential to company development but they need managerial commitment to carry them through. The informed manager *is* the key, not only to a strong internal communication strategy but to a comprehensive involvement in company policy which is reflected out to the institutional investor, the financial analyst, the pressure group member, the politician and the shopper in the supermarket.

As a newly appointed communication manager I was balancing my company lunch tray between the canteen tables when a colleague strode by. 'Hello, Peter', he chirped, 'still communicating like mad?'

He'd missed the point entirely. It is not – and never has been – the job of specialist communicators, whether in-house or consulting, to personally carry through the company's job of communication. That task is firmly pinned to the chest of every manager in the business.

The informed manager

These managers – and perhaps you are among them – need to

be informed and need to be helped to inform others by practical training and assessment. They need the confidence that can only be given them by direct communication from the Top Men; they also need to be given the means and the training to enable them to communicate corporate messages to their immediate employees and to those outside, including Press, distributors, franchise holders, customers, prospective employees and executives in other companies.

If commitment comes from the top, then

ACTION MUST COME FROM THE CENTRE

How that action takes place and what help can be given is a subject for a later chapter but at this stage let me echo the findings of Warren Bennis in a survey of leadership behaviour in some of America's best-run companies.

He concluded that it's unlikely that line managers will perform well unless they feel 'ownership' for their work. It is such 'ownership' that managers need to feel over the communication network and which all too often has been prised from their grasp by the chief executive above and by the office and shop floor below.

This, then, is the communicating management inside the company from whom and through whom any controlled, corporate communication programme must evolve and flow:

▷ The chief executive and the board who must provide commitment to communication while recognising the need for delegation.

▷ **The centre wedge of senior and middle management who must be prepared to carry the communication policies through, both internally and externally.**

There is the Company. Here are the Communicators who work for it. Now we must move beyond the corporate structure and consider just who it is that we need to communicate with. Who are the Audiences?

4
Audiences unlimited

Smiling in the rain

ON A DAMP NOVEMBER morning in 1984, five men stood on a London rooftop for a press photocall. Photographers squeezed around the service ducts, jostling for the best viewpoint, and in the next morning's newspapers the City quintet, smiling despite the drizzle, appeared beneath headlines proclaiming MASSIVE OVERSUBSCRIPTION and MILLIONS OF FIRST-TIME BUYERS.

The famous five included the Chairman and Deputy Chairman of British Telecom and in the background a vivid yellow banner topped the office roof of merchant bankers Kleinwort Benson, proclaiming a share price of 130p. That photocall was one of the final stages of the run-in to what was called at the time 'The biggest flotation in history' – the privatisation of British Telecom.

The campaign had started in July the previous year with the first meeting of the flotation public relations sub-committee. It ended seventeen months later when BT shares were traded for the first time on the London, New York and Toronto Stock Exchanges.

☆ ☆ ☆

THIS CORPORATE COMMUNICATION programme was a remarkable and award-winning achievement. However, it is not the sheer size of the operation which is of interest here (a massive 650,000 telephone enquiries and 730,000 letters were handled during the campaign), but the many and varied audiences which must be communicated with if such a corporate communication exercise is to succeed. In the BT flotation programme these included trade unions, customers, Members of Parliament, pressure groups and opinion formers, the general public, the financial analysts and, most importantly, the workforce, whose acceptance of the scheme was crucial to its success.

British Telecom and its professional advisers had a basic communication task – they were simply aiming to arouse positive interest and encourage the participation of every person in the United Kingdom in the rebirth of a company.

But that is not always the case. According to Sir Peter Parker, Chairman of Rockware,

> 'Increasingly, Boards of British industry are aware of their cat's cradle of criss-cross, often contradictory responsibilities to customer, community, shareholders and employees; and of the awkward allocation of corporate resources to cope with this baffling balance of obligations. And in the emerging range of such questions, very much at the heart of them is another question; do we invest adequate money and thought in communications to try to fulfil the role of modern management in meeting its fourfold responsibilities? The effectiveness of boards in their own performance across the full span of communications is not to be taken glibly for granted.'

Yes, the company's communication responsibilities are often a cat's cradle, for the audiences with whom we wish to communicate vary so much in what they demand and how we wish to influence them. Who are they and what do they want of us?

The employees – appreciation or apathy?

One of British Telecom's major tasks was to tell its workforce the facts about the changes in the company and to counter unease caused by fundamental shifts in regulatory policy and varying interpretations of Government intentions. The message was conveyed to the 240,000 staff that what may have been perceived as a twin-headed monster actually provided a challenge which, if realised, would ensure a glittering future. A programme of personal letters from BT's Chairman, Sir George Jefferson, was mailed to each employee's home; two special editions of the house newspaper were published and a ten-minute commercial was screened on *TV-am* aimed both to reassure and inform staff and customers alike.

The positive response from the BT workforce (96 per cent actually became shareholders in the new business) is not shared by all white and blue collar staff in their relations with the company and its management. In the United States, for all the rhetoric in popular management books, employee surveys indicate that the workforce thinks management is doing a *poorer* job of communicating with them than it did five years before. The source is a survey of 48,000 employees by Opinion Research Corporation.

Downward communication, measured by employees' ratings of their companies on letting them know what is going on, is rated favourably by fewer than *half* of employees in all groups.

Commenting on the situation in *Fortune*, consultant Walter Kiechel writes:

'*If the brass don't wake up soon, they stand to get their sleepy little heads handed to them by the competition. Virtually everyone who has studied the problem – executives, consultants, business school professors – agrees that you have to share lots of information with employees if you hope to elicit their commitment. Commitment, the latest emerging buzzword, means high productivity, low turnover, and a better chance of avoiding corporate death at the hands of the Japanese.'*

Kiechel goes on:

'So why don't more executives get off the mute, inglorious dime? Partly because they haven't wanted to be the bearers of bad news – the global competition is killing us, we're being taken over, you've just lost in the downsizing lottery.'

But, he concludes, good times or bad, workers these days expect *more* information on what's happening to the company and how it will affect them. Managers are too ready to believe that they have responded to these heightened expectations when they haven't. What is needed is to talk more – all the way down the line and, after all the talking, to show that what you heard makes a difference.

Take the money and run

There is a similar picture in the UK where a MORI survey, published in 1986 (ironically, Britain's Industry Year), canvassed more than 1,000 workers in a wide spread of industrial life: private companies, local government, retail, national government, self-employed, nationalised industries and professional organisations. By comparison with a similar survey ten years before, workers were now far more interested in pay and job security, far less interested in having a boss they respected and a say in how the work was done. Most shop floor workers were satisfied with their jobs but satisfaction was falling, they felt less informed and their distrust of company information had grown. The overall feeling, no doubt aggravated by a jumpy national economy and the high level of unemployment, seemed to be to take the money and run while you've got the chance.

The Sunday Times reported on the survey:

> '*T*he sad truth is probably ... that if there has been a change in shop floor workers' relationships with management it stems largely from a fear of unemployment...
>
> 'This undoubtedly helps keep shopfloor grievances under control and moderates pay ambitions – not so much a positive revolution in attitudes as a sterile stalemate.
>
> 'But what will happen if unemployment falls? Will the shop floor's distrust of management and its pent-up frustrations spill over into a new, and damaging, wave of industrial militancy? The evidence of our survey suggests that it easily might.'

Yet despite this gloomy picture from the US and the UK the employees *do* still care about the company they work for. When asked *what* they want to know about the company, the order of priority is overwhelmingly about:

▷ **The organisation's future plans.**
▷ **The organisation's competitive position.**

> ▷ **Job advancement opportunities.**
> ▷ **Productivity improvement.**

Those old palliatives of promotions, retirements and obituaries, those cosy human interest stories about other employees, and news of what the company is doing in the community, are way down at the bottom of the list.

The demand for information has moved strongly in recent years from the established, comfortable facts of the past to the tenuous, uncomfortable predictions about the next six months. The assessment of this particular corporate audience is essentially that there is

EXPECTATION FROM BELOW

Don't forget the unions

When union communication arises it is often parcelled without further thought into Personnel or Industrial Relations. But communication with the unions should be part of the corporate communication programme, closely linked as it is with the employee-related group. Union members and, particularly, union organisers at local and national level are a key audience.

An attitude survey was being conducted among a random selection of chemical industry employees throughout the British Isles. All seemed to be going well until the assessors arrived at a northern site to run the day's interviews, only to be told that the assignment was off. The majority union at the plant had not been consulted about the survey, felt that it was probing too deeply into the attitudes of its members towards the company and had instructed its members not to cooperate. That important segment of the company had to be abandoned and the total effectiveness of the project was reduced.

The lesson is plain: if your company is unionised, then those unions and their members must be one of your audiences. And within that audience must also come the participators – those employees (often union shop stewards) who represent employees on joint consultative councils or wider participation schemes. In one respect they are insiders, with an inbuilt loyalty to the company, but in another they are outsiders, struggling to maintain an uneasy compromise between allegiance and criticism.

Perhaps you feel that union members already have enough information! It's true that legislation in Western Europe since the early 1970s has given union negotiators much key information as a right, but simply passing out sheets of words and figures is not communication: there has to be a two-way or preferably a three-way process. Communication by the company to its audiences must be a vertical two-way flow but there must also be a lateral exchange of views if the communication triangle is to be complete.

The customer – still king?

Almost every company has customers: those to whom it sells products or provides services, whether they are a queue of shoppers at a supermarket checkout or the assembled cabinet of a foreign government. What is it that customers want?

Obviously they want the right product or service at the right price at the right time. But over and above this basic equation are those intangible aspects which determine final choice and which are all part of the corporate communication programme. There may be little to choose between one fast food chain and the next, between the major clearing banks, between estate agents Alpha and Omega. Similar products and similar services – yet somehow we all have to make a decision.

In a research study commissioned by consultants Valin Pollen, respondents were asked what selection factors were used in determining the choice of a property consultant. The results were:

Reputation	32%
Market knowledge	24%
Quality of service	20%
Geographical spread	10%

If customers are looking primarily to reputation as a guide, those intangibles which make up the public image of the company must be a prime concern of the company's board and management.

The customer must be convinced by what he reads, sees and hears about the company that it has a reputation he can trust, and when he has direct contact with its products and services – at any level – he must find a matching experience, a mirror image.

For example, early in 1986 British Rail launched a massive campaign to convince its customers that it was moving onto new tracks, switching to a more efficient line of service.

Television commercials showed trains running on time, porters appearing to assist luggage-laden passengers and ticket collectors benevolently directing little boys lost. This was all underwritten by the proud boast that thousands of staff had attended customer-liaison training sessions and that British Rail was now 'getting there'.

The reaction from BR customers in conversation and in print was a mixture of annoyance and ridicule. Trains were still late, staff unhelpful, carriages uncleaned, announcements incoherent. The advertised benefits were clearly not up to customer expectation and the company's reputation suffered. There was no mirror image – only a rather grubby reflection.

Today, with less and less to choose between competing products and services, customers demand an honest assessment of what they are about to receive and, due to the efforts in the UK and the US of the consumer-protection groups, they are no longer hoodwinked by the twin masks of size and history. They demand comprehensive information quickly and in words and formats they can understand. Crucially, they need to be told, **the truth**. The customer is still king (or queen) and has a right to know.

Pity the small investor

Flotations in the 1980s such as British Telecom, TSB, British Gas and British Airways have rapidly increased the number of small private shareholders. But even before these flotations, the demands of shareholders for increased width and detail in company information had been recognised as a growing need to be satisfied. The BT exercise was concerned with creating new shareholders (they achieved 2.4 million founders). Existing publically-quoted companies, on the other hand, need to keep theirs and make sure that, like the customers, they are fully informed and have complete confidence in a strong and resilient reputation.

After a dawn raid in the City, the chairman of a company which had been taken over was heard to remark plaintively that he hadn't even had a chance of talking to his shareholders. In fact he had had innumerable opportunities which he had simply squandered. Shareholders are one of the most captive of the audiences with whom we have to communicate; their names are known, their addresses are filed, they already have an intrinsic interest in our company.

So often in the past it has been assumed that the company investor is merely concerned with an annual and interim report and the opportunity to ask a question or scramble for a quick gin and tonic at the Annual Meeting. The needs of the individual shareholder have often been overshadowed by the more grandiose demands of the institutional shareholders and the City analysts.

As Eric Silvester, the British Oxygen Company's former investor relations manager, points out:

'*Of course, it is true that the institutional investors do wield enormous power. But I think many investor relations managers feel that one of our functions should be to stimulate interest in equity investment among as broad a cross-section of the public as possible.*'

Sir Nicholas Goodison, Chairman of the London Stock Exchange, feels that there needs to be a vital understanding between listed companies and their shareholders that allows the shareholders both to manage their risk effectively, and to feel sufficiently involved in a company's progress to want to give their whole-hearted support to its managers.

A passion for detail

While the company must consider the growing demands of the private shareholders, it must not neglect those of the institutional shareholders, the merchant banks and the stockbrokers' analysts. These audiences are crucial to the building and maintenance of that aspect of the company we have already identified as central to the corporate goals – its reputation.

These groups have an insatiable appetite for everything about your company – not only its trading figures (in the greatest detail) but its products, markets, management, plant and employees. These are important audiences; not only because of the power and influence they wield at the financial hub of industry but because an open dialogue established between the company and these groups can give vital information to the chief executive and directors on how the company is viewed and what future steps will find favour with the City.

Such a tradition is of recent date in the UK, where the Investor Relations Society held its inaugural meeting in 1980 and now has 150 members, but in the US investor relations are more advanced, with the National Investor Relations Institute having 1,400 members.

This growing professionalism of specialist investor communication should be reflected in the attitude of company boards. The spate of actual and attempted takeovers in the past few years should have alerted every public company to the fact that an annual chat round the boardroom dining table is only the starting point for communication with the City – not the conclusion.

Support your local Member

Much of the BT campaign thrust was towards Westminster – naturally enough as the company was moving out of the control of Government into privatisation.

A programme of contact with Parliamentarians and opinion formers was evolved to influence decisions over the potential splitting-up of BT and excessive regulation, and to ensure a clear perception of the company's stance during the legislative period. With all-night sittings it was often a 24-hour operation for the communication team.

This was a special case but for any company the governmental group should be recognised and communicated with – whether this involves loaning the company offices for evening meetings of the local council like one Southampton manufacturer, or mounting a major information campaign aimed at the heart of Westminster, Washington or Brussels.

Nigel Rowe, in *Communicate* (1977):

'The role of government in shaping the policies and performances of business enterprise is a growing concern for management around the world. It is perhaps especially true of Europe, where government plays a more direct role than virtually anywhere outside the Iron

> *Curtain. Indeed, many chief executives in Europe see the increasing involvement of government, growing out of social and environmental pressures and the perceived needs of national economies, as the single most challenging problem for the future.*'

Much of our corporate communication programme is not concerned with audiences *en masse* but with individuals within those audiences – and this is particularly so with government. As an impartial, faceless administration, government will demand certain information and action from the company which the company is obliged to give.

But outside those legislative demands – and far more important – is how we communicate with the Members of Parliament and local politicians who are linked by location or political interest with our factories and offices or our particular areas of business. We need their help and influence – or may need it in the future – and they in turn may be glad of our expert advice when computers or frozen food or holiday travel or whatever our specialisation is becomes a matter for national debate. We need to establish a working relationship – a dialogue. Nor should we forget the permanent civil servants in government departments where good relations can be built up over many years, irrespective of who holds the strings of political power at Westminster.

The eyes of the world

Standing at the back of the circle of onlookers and totally ignored by many companies is the largest and most amorphous group of them all – the General Public.

They were certainly not ignored in the flotation programme by British Telecom, who needed to reposition the company in the public eye. The urgent task was to demonstrate that the Civil Service ethos had been swept away, BT had really changed for the better, and that the services it offered were innovative and more varied than those of its competitors. For the first time, BT undertook an image-raising programme, the main thrust being the 'Power behind the Button' series of advertisements which monthly research later confirmed had successfully improved BT's public profile.

Yes, the public *are* important. Thanks to the electronic media, they are now international judge and jury on our affairs; and whether it's an explosion at one of our chemical plants, the injection of cyanide into a batch of our pharmaceuticals or the filling of our chocolate bars with heroin, our company will be wide open to the eyes and ears of the world.

And remember that the general public is not just a faceless mass of ciphers to be tabulated into categories A, B or C for marketing exercises. It is made up of small groups of individuals – customers, political party members, shareholders, graduates, employees ... even managers! Elsewhere we have discussed (and will discuss again) the communication needs of these audiences and, believe it or not,

THESE ARE THE SAME PEOPLE

A simple message but one which some managements seem resolved to ignore.

So it is no use telling your customers one thing through an

expensive advertising campaign if they read the opposite in their evening paper. It is pointless trying to convince your employees that prospects are good and the workforce is happy if a television news programme interviews disgruntled shop stewards and reports an empty order book. The same message must be understood by the general audience as well as by the particular. Even if your communication strategy demands a programme of audience briefing which gives one group more information than another, the basic facts must be the same.

All groups great and small

There are many smaller audiences whose existence in the corporate communication plan depends on what the company does, where it operates and who it's owned by.

For manufacturing and retailing companies, the particular communication needs of suppliers, franchisees, distributors and dealers must be carefully considered, particularly as many of these audiences have a direct and crucial link with customers and the general public.

For those in the chemical industry, in meat, furs, dairy produce, tobacco, glass and metal containers and other vulnerable commodities, the particular pressure group must be recognised and communicated with.

▷ **For those with factories and offices in residential and rural areas, the local community will figure strongly in their corporate programme.**
▷ **For large companies with a demand for high level**

executives and managers with particular skills, graduates – and the institutions behind them – will be an important audience.

▷ For major industrial companies and associations the needs of schoolteachers, college and university lecturers and their students will have to be recognised.

▷ And for almost all organisations the growing influence of those who have retired, both as company pensioners and in the community at large, must be remembered.

All these audiences, great and small, have some part to play in the company's outreach towards the pursuit of achieving its aims and objectives and explaining its policies and achievements.

They are all linked to one of the four audience groups: employee-related, product-related, finance-related and government-related, but their individual needs vary. What they can do for the company and its reputation varies, but they must first be recognised for what they are, they must be given the information and the contacts appropriate to their needs and

THEY MUST BE TOLD THE TRUTH.

We have yet to discuss what we are going to say to these disparate groups and, just as important, how we are going to get the message across. But unless from the start we are determined to treat them as we would be treated ourselves, we are pursuing a downhill road and our cat's cradle of communication will become hopelessly tangled.

On the subject of company integrity, the authors of *The Winning Streak* say:

> '*The reverse side of the coin is that all of these audiences ... tend to return the compliment, treating the company with the integrity it demands of them.*'

So, accept that your company management has a large number of audiences to deal with; each with different needs, each with different benefits for you if they are correctly approached.

List them: the employees, trade unionists, pensioners, graduates; the customers, dealers, suppliers, distributors, general public, action groups; the small and institutional shareholders, banks, investment analysts; the local and county councils, MPs, local community, government departments, educationalists.

They demand – and deserve – an honest, controlled (not contrived) communication programme about your company. And, above all, when dealing with them, remember always that

INTEGRITY IS INTEGRAL.

We have looked at the Company, at those Communicators who work for it and at the groups of individuals, the Audiences, who wait outside. The next question is: what have they got to say to each other?

5
Something to say

We are not amused

OLD STORIES are sometimes the best. None could be more appropriate when discussing communication than to picture again one of the technological achievements of Victorian Britain: the inauguration of the telegraph line to India.

The year is 1860. The equipment which will send a message from the Queen's ministers to the people of India, 4,000 miles across the globe, is explained and praised, but Queen Victoria is not amused.

'That is all very well,' she is reported to have said. 'But what exactly have my ministers to *say* to the people of India?'

THAT IS CLOSE to the knuckle at this stage of our exploration of corporate communication. What exactly *has* our company to say to its audiences?

Before we answer that question let us look at the story so far. We have pictured the company as a ball of solid facts and hot air spinning through inter-corporate space. Let's continue that planetary analogy.

On a slow-moving inner ring next to the centre is the crucial band of individuals whose job it is to do the communicating. Here they all are, separated by years of experience, by job function, by salary and location, and by cubic centimetre of car engine; but all bound together by tenuous strands of varying strength and flexibility, ranging from the IBM-style corporate culture loyalty to that most basic common denominator – a salary cheque from the same computer.

These, I have suggested, should be the Communicators: the

Top Man, whether chairman, president, chief executive or managing director; the non-executive directors; the directors or vice-presidents; the divisional directors or executives, both at home and abroad; the senior and middle managers, concerned individually with production or finance or human resources, but all corporately concerned with that central core of information at the heart of the system.

Out on the fringe, whirling faster and sometimes difficult to identify in the mist, are those who by choice or chance are influenced by the company and who can influence the company in their turn. These are the general and specialist audiences of the last chapter.

And at the core of this concentric pattern are the hard facts of company life: corporate policies, corporate objectives and corporate achievements – something like the futuristic sketch on the opposite page.

The media are not the message

It is at this point that we echo Victoria and ask, not 'Is anybody there?' (there most certainly is!) but 'Have we anything to say?' In that question VRI shrewdly anticipated a management trap which has grown in size and complexity from her time through the publication boom of the fifties and sixties and the video bandwagon of the seventies, on to the Information Technology morass of the eighties in which many companies are in danger of sinking up to their megabytes in hard and software.

The media *are* important but they are *not* the message, and before we attempt to evaluate *how* to communicate across the

*'... the company as a ball of solid
facts and hot air spinning
through inter-corporate space.'*

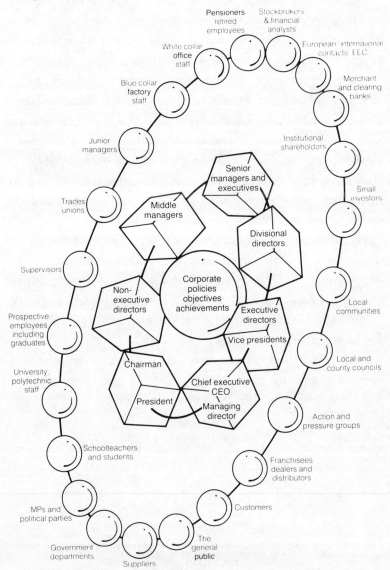

corporate divide we must try to establish a general pattern of *what* to communicate.

For so many companies on both sides of the Atlantic, the accepted approach to communication is *re*-active. They develop a piecemeal policy which majors on a defensive approach to relations with employees, Press, customers, financial analysts, Government, unions and, sometimes, even shareholders.

Every request for information is weighed, measured and debated and the bare minimum supplied. And so when disaster looms and the strike or the attempted takeover or the plant explosion forces them into the glare of unwelcome publicity, they have nothing to offer but a second-rate annual report, an out-dated list of City editors and a hastily written and ill-judged press statement.

What they *should* be doing – what *your* company should be doing – is to start developing a *pro*-active communication programme which will examine the messages coming out of the central core and, by channelling them to the right audience in the right manner at the right time, gain maximum support for the company objectives.

And if we look at the messages within a broad-based corporate communication programme we find they will helpfully slot into three collection boxes labelled:

ENFORCED

EXPECTED

EXPEDIENT

Look at these groupings as they apply to your own company.

The *enforced* information is that which you have no choice but to communicate; it is laid down in Section V, sub-section ii, paragraph 6(a) of some Government directive; it is part of a printed contract or it is a condition of trade or service.

The *expected* information ebbs and flows with the current industrial, political and social climate. It is what is expected of us as a fair-minded, level-headed, efficient company by each of our audiences.

The *expedient* information is what many companies would *like* to use to construct their entire communication programme. It is those messages which *we* want to put across to help achieve our objectives.

Enforced – the writing on the label

The weight of information which the company must disclose by law becomes heavier each year. Products for sale must not only conform to manufacturing specifications but must pass on much of that information to the potential buyer, whether it is the percentage of polyester in a bedsheet or the fact that a packet of mushroom soup contains sodium phosphates, carob gum, monosodium glutamate, hydrolysed protein, starch and sodium caseinate.

Now, much of this type of information will be handled as routine procedure by the departments concerned within the inner corporate ring, whether R & D, Production, Finance or Quality Control. But there are two particular areas of enforced communication which every manager should be aware of and they are those which affect two significant audiences – the employees and the shareholders.

In the late 1970s those involved in employee communication were slipping the catchwords 'Vredeling' and 'the Fifth Directive' into their management backchat. These were not draft titles for a brace of pulp spy thrillers but much-debated draft legislation from the EEC which would force member countries to adopt measures of employee participation (such as worker director boards), which have proved too far-reaching for some members – including the UK – to accept.

The Rt Hon Tom King, when Secretary of State for Employment, made this clear in *Industrial Society*:

> '*It is vital for our future economic prosperity that we concentrate strongly on employee involvement. But it is better achieved by building up goodwill and trust rather than being directed with rules and regulations. Those companies which already follow this do not need to be told of the benefits and value to all – to individuals, businesses and to the country as a whole. It is the ones which lag behind that need to be reached.*'

And for the laggards, Section 1 of the Employment Act of 1982, enforces all companies with more than 250 employees to include in their annual directors' report a statement of what action has been taken during the year to introduce, maintain or develop arrangements to:

▷ **provide employees systematically with information of matters of concern to them as employees;**
▷ **consult them or their representatives on a regular basis so that their views can be taken into account**

in making decisions which are likely to affect their
interests;
▷ encourage their involvement in the company's
performance through an employee share scheme
or by some other means;
▷ achieve a common awareness on the part of all
employees of the financial and economic factors
affecting the performance of the company.

We have already noted that companies are also required by law
to provide properly appointed trades union representatives
with any information they require about the company's
finances which is considered relevant to negotiation.

No palliatives please

In all of this there is still obviously a need for a measure of
goodwill from the companies. Like the now hackneyed
paragraph in annual reports about the company's willingness
to employ disabled staff, the 'communication paragraph' could
easily become an equally hackneyed and meaningless palliative
to those demanding increased worker participation.

So far as the shareholder is concerned, this is not likely to
happen. The facts and figures which must be put into an
annual report and accounts are finely detailed and getting
longer by the year.

As more British companies take an interest in launching out
in the United States, even more detail becomes necessary and
the stringent requirements of quarterly reporting have to be
followed. And as smaller companies move onto the Unlisted

Securities Market so they find themselves forced in their placing documents to put down on paper and publish to the world many facts and figures of which they were hardly aware themselves.

Such enforcement can be beneficial in the long run – but it can never go far enough.

Accountants Arthur Young, in their paper *Sharing the Facts*, state:

> '*Quality of information is far more important than quantity, as any manager would agree. Besides, the* disclosure *of information is not the same as its* communication. *To be communicated, the information must be understood. The annual report, to take an obvious example, is presented largely in accounting terminology, often unintelligible to most people except in very general terms. A technical accounting document is essential for the important but comparatively small number of people – bankers, financial analysts, institutional investors – directly concerned with company finances. But many annual reports do not meet the real information needs of the other users – shareholders, employees, consumers, local communities, the general public – who constitute the majority of those affected by company activities.*'

So let us all be aware and regularly informed on what information is currently enforced but please don't let's assume that meeting the current legislative demands can be accepted as effective corporate communication. And if you doubt that, just look at the next cigarette advertisement that comes your way and note how the enforced strip of black type at the foot of the poster (always in the same typeface) is totally overwhelmed by the broad bands of colour extolling the product itself. No, dissemination is *not* communication.

Expected – the writing on the wall

Companies are seldom criticised for not meeting their legal obligations in passing on information. They *are* frequently criticised for not communicating what can be reasonably *expected* of them in a given situation.

James Wilkinson wrote in *The Listener* following the Chernobyl crisis:

> '*When the radioactive cloud reached Britain a week after the accident, there was little appreciation by the Government of the degree of concern among ordinary people or of what their response to that concern should be.*'

Exactly. A large part of the whole sad story of that nuclear accident was not scientific incompetence but the failure to communicate the information that people *expected* to be told, from official bodies monitoring radiation levels to dairy farmers checking their milk yields.

To appreciate exactly *what* people expect (and every audience will expect slightly different facts and figures) the company, and its professional advisers, must blend psychology and methodology. They must put themselves into the minds of their disparate audiences and ask, 'If I were them, what would I reasonably expect to know?' But because this may require a greater effort of will or imagination than some of us possess, they must also *ask* people what they expect through controlled market research. The scope and range of that research may be deep and broad – from informal discussion in the works canteen to monthly opinion soundings from a select number of analysts on a City panel – but it will produce an essential core of information which we can be reasonably certain is expected of our company.

As an example – and moving to an area which is familiar to all company managers – what do the employee audiences want to know about their company? What do they expect?

Here are 17 subjects on which employees might be expected to want more information. Why not rate them in the order in which *you* think employees in your company would agree in their expectations:

SUBJECTS OF INTEREST

1 The organisation's stand on current issues.
2 How my job fits into the organisation.
3 News of other departments/divisions.
4 Financial results.
5 Personnel policies and practices.
6 Human interest stories about other employees.
7 Personnel changes/promotions.
8 Organisation's competitive position.
9 Productivity improvement.
10 Personnel news (birthdays, anniversaries etc).
11 Effect of external events on my job.
12 Organisation's future plans.
13 Job advancement opportunities.
14 Job-related information.
15 Organisation's community involvement.
16 Advertising and promotional plans.
17 How the organisation uses its profits.

The most recent of the two-year rolling surveys conducted by the International Association of Business Communicators with Towers, Perrin, Forster & Crosby, covering 10,000 employees in ten companies, revealed the following order of expectation:

RANKING	Very interested in receiving further information
1 Organisation's future plans	79.8%
2 Job advancement opportunities	72.5%
3 Job-related information	68.0%
4 Productivity improvement	63.0%
5 Personnel policies and practices	62.8%
6 Organisation's competitive position	62.7%
7 How my job fits into the organisation	62.1%
8 Effect of external events on my job	52.9%
9 How the organisation uses its profit	48.6%
10 Financial results	44.1%
11 Advertising and promotional plans	43.4%
12 News of other departments/divisions	43.3%
13 Organisation's stand on current issues	42.7%
14 Personnel changes/promotions	41.1%
15 Organisation's community involvement	39.3%
16 Human interest stories about other employees	21.6%
17 Personnel news (birthdays, anniversaries etc)	16.0%

Establishing what information *is* expected may make the communication challenge ahead more difficult rather than easier. In this case it seems that the main desire of employees is for more details on what the company is planning for its (and, ultimately, their) future and what the competition is up to – invariably two of the most difficult topics on which to prise information from the company hierarchy.

Nevertheless, establishing what *kind* of information slots into the *expected* category is necessary and vital and such a process applies equally to *all* the corporate audiences: whether they are prospective graduate managers or probing investment analysts. What do they expect? That is the question.

Expedient – we are the greatest

Cassius Clay, in his butterfly days, developed a succinct mission statement and punched it home until the phrase became synonymous with the man.

Within that central core of our corporate policies, objectives and achievements are those things which we wish others to understand about our company. They will probably not be as simplistic or bombastic as 'We are the greatest!' but they will need to be sorted and stated before they can be rammed home with the same sting and precision.

Unlike the *enforced* and *expected* messages we cannot refer to external sources. This is the time when the management communicators have to examine themselves and their company and ask basic and, sometimes, self-evident questions such as

WHO ARE WE?

WHAT DO WE STAND FOR?

WHERE ARE WE GOING?

The actual information which backs up these basic statements will vary from time to time but the overall messages should be consistent. For some companies the essential messages will be those contained in the usual preamble to the annual report, such as this brief mission statement from the Burton Group:

> *The Group's mission is to become Britain's top fashion retailer, both for clothing and the home. We aim to create a wider personal choice for our customers as their individual needs and aspirations change. We intend to continue to improve benefits for shareholders, customers and employees.*
>
> *The Group is committed in all its retail formats to creating a brighter High Street, and widening consumer choice in terms of products, services and retail environments. Customers demand variety, quality and value for money. The Group will continue to meet this demand by developing attractive, appropriate retail formulae for its wide range of target markets.*

For other companies a detailed analysis of corporate belief and direction will be contained in a mission statement leaflet. The somewhat flashy title of this document may discourage the more traditional companies from using it. They should overcome their natural reserve because it is a most useful communication tool and the very process of putting the facts we want to communicate down on paper will help us to concentrate on the essential purposes of the corporation.

For example, prior to a conference of world-wide executives, Cadbury Schweppes issued a leaflet entitled *The Character of the Company* setting out its *expedient* information. The section headings and a sample quotation provide a useful guide to the type of information which may be considered in this third category:

---

1 *Competitive ability* – 'Cadbury Schweppes must be competitive in the market place.'
2 *Clear objectives* – 'effective competition demands clarity of purpose.'
3 *Taking advantage of change* – 'The aim is to encourage openness to new ideas and a readiness to adapt to changing needs.'
4 *Simple organisation* – 'all decisions should be taken as near their point of impact as possible.'
5 *Committed people* – 'the company is made up of individuals and its success turns on their collective commitment to its aims.'
6 *Openness* – 'openness and trust are the basis of good working relationships.'
7 *Responsibility* – 'the company recognises its obligations to all who have a stake in its success and seeks to keep its responsibilities to them in balance.'
8 *Quality* – 'the quality we aim for in all our dealings is that of integrity: the word integrity means straight dealing but it also means completeness.'

In a conclusion to this leaflet, chairman Sir Adrian Cadbury points a warning for those companies who believe that communication is achieved by just publishing such a list:

'*Cadbury Schweppes'* concern for the values I have described will not be judged by this statement, but by our actions.'

What to communicate

So let us be aware that before we *begin* to communicate with those designated audiences out in inter-corporate space, we must establish just what it is that we need to communicate.

We need to communicate facts, figures and the expression of values and beliefs, taken from our corporate policies, objectives and achievements.

 We need to assess that information in three main areas:

ENFORCED – what has been *legislated for us* by forces outside our control.

EXPECTED – what it is that *our audiences want to know* (within reason); which we must research to discover.

EXPEDIENT – what *we want to communicate* about our own company for others to understand.

These are the *messages*. The *media* which we will use to put them across the gap between us and our *audiences* are the subject of the next three chapters.

6
Face to face

Communication as she is spoken

AN INTERVIEWER was gathering information for a survey conducted by accountants Touche Ross.

It was a hot day in Yorkshire and the interviewee was a sweating, muscular furnaceman, obviously aggrieved at being questioned. He answered patiently, however, and the questioner finally summoned sufficient courage to ask him if he had understood the financial information in the company's printed annual report.

The furnaceman thought for a moment and then said, 'Aye, I understand it ... but what does it *mean?*'

IT IS NOT UNTIL we get face to face with our audiences that we are in a position to answer such questions, say what things mean and correct the errors in our preconceptions of people's information needs. But such an approach does not always find favour with the company communicators.

'Whenever I hear the word "communication"', say far too many Top Men, 'I reach for my video camera.'

Well, the electronic media have a right and proper place in the modern communication armoury but the first thing any manager should reach for is not the latest audio-visual gimmick but the oldest communication medium of all – speech. Why? Because it is *still* the medium that most people, like the furnaceman, prefer.

In the last chapter we looked at the IABC/TPF&C survey on employee communication trends. It is only one of many available surveys in the communication field, covering many audiences, but it gives significant help on this particular topic. It looks at the media through which 10,000 employes would *prefer* to receive information rather than those through which they *actually* receive it.

What are respondents' major preferred and current sources of organisational information?

Preferred			Current	
Ranking	Major source for:	Source of information	Ranking	Major source for:
1	92.3%	My immediate supervisor	1	59.7%
2	63.0%	Small group meetings	3	33.1%
3	55.5%	Top executives	10	13.3%
4	45.8%	Annual state-of-the-business report	8	16.8%
5	41.2%	Employee handbook/ brochures	5	26.6%
6	41.1%	Orientation programme	11	12.9%
7	40.4%	Local employee publication	7	19.2%
8	38.5%	Organisation-wide employee publication	6	21.2%
9	37.1%	Bulletin boards	4	30.1%
10	33.8%	Upward communication programme	15	9.1%
11	30.3%	Mass meetings	9	16.6%
12	23.2%	Audio-visual programmes	14	9.3%
13	20.4%	The union	12	12.3%
14	10.5%	The grapevine	2	40.4%
15	8.8%	Mass media	13	10.5%

We see a clear preference for face-to-face communication: with immediate supervisors, in small group meetings and in meetings with top executives. Audio-visual programmes, despite being the flavour of the month in many large organisations, are low in this preference table – and that preference is typical of the UK, the US and Canada.

Perhaps this preference for face-to-face contact stems from the fact that in these difficult times for industry and business, people need *personal* reassurance. Their belief in the credibility of the written word and the visual image may well have been dented and, like the furnaceman, they welcome the opportunity of the face-to-face meeting where questions can be asked and assessments made.

From the company viewpoint, it is often not until we talk face to face with the customer or the investor or the dealer that we are able to gain for ourselves that most valuable ingredient of any communication process – *feedback*.

One to one – the personal interview

Time and again in current management books extolling excellence, successful Top Men preach the virtues of the factory or branch walkabout. Sir John Sainsbury, the top brass at Marks and Spencer, the Mars brothers, all advocate the benefits of personal contact and discussion with their employees. Goldsmith and Clutterbuck record how Lord Sieff, Chairman of Marks and Spencer until his retirement in 1984, put the spoken word into practice.

'*On one occasion near to retirement, when very heavy snowfalls had blocked most main roads, he still insisted on driving from London all the way down to Chatham, just to thank the sales assistants for turning up in spite of the weather. A telephone call would have sufficed to pass on the content of the message but the only way to put across the genuine appreciation that top management felt was to go there and tell people in person.*

'Sieff's weekly routine included telephone calls every Saturday at around five pm to four or five stores chosen at random, to check on how the day's trading had gone. To the branch managers contacted in this way without warning it was a valuable reminder that top management really was interested in their progress.'

But the one-to-one interview does not only apply when dealing with an employee audience. Personal interviews with graduates in their role of potential employees, with leading stockbrokers' analysts, with editors and journalists, with Members of Parliament, civil servants, local councillors, action group chairmen ... the list is long. Wherever it *can* be done there is no better way to communicate specific information and gain an original viewpoint.

But, as with any communication medium, there are hazards – of misinterpretation, of misunderstanding, of misreporting. To avoid these, the interviewer should aim to build in a number of reinforcements.

▷ **Start with a written outline of what you want to say.**
▷ **Make sure the person you are talking with has an opportunity for questions, and *actively* encourage**

him or her to ask for an explanation of anything that has not been completely understood.

▷ Confirm any agreement made or decisions to be taken *in writing* immediately after the discussion and ensure that the written message itself is received and confirmed as being understood.

Face-to-face dialogue (and it should never be a monologue) is an excellent way to communicate if efficiently used but if the back-up safety net of some kind of written report is ignored then all too soon the air is full of: 'I don't remember that ...', 'I'm sure you didn't say that' or, worse, 'Well, it's your word against mine, old boy.'

One to several – the briefing group

For managers in British industry the very name *briefing group* has become synonymous with the Industrial Society which, during John Garnett's 30 years as Director, made this technique, now known as *team briefing*, the foundation of its communication gospel. But a briefing group is also the White House press conference, or the managing director's annual pep talk to the North of England reps, or the chairman's quarterly chat to the City analysts. In each case the guiding factor is that the information is intended to be passed on: by the line manager to his supervisors; by the journalist to his readers, listeners or viewers; by the representative to his customers.

As with one-to-one interviews, the briefing group can be a reliable method of communicating information but only if its several criteria are met.

▷ *Numbers* must not be too large to prevent every person – even the most reticent – from having the opportunity to ask questions. This suggests a maximum of about twenty.

▷ *Timing* is crucial, whether to enable the journalist to leave in time to meet his copy deadline or to allow the machine shop to get their lunch before the canteen closes.

▷ *The speaker* must be fully briefed and trained not only to communicate facts, figures and policy statements but to respond intelligently to questions, either with an immediate answer or by promising to find out the information after the meeting.

▷ *The group members* must be provided with briefing notes summarising the information communicated. This will usually be typed or printed, in perhaps a duplicated briefing sheet, a press release or an illustrated leaflet, but in some cases may be an audio or video cassette. It must be assumed that *every* member of a briefing group is a potential carrier of information and will brief others in their turn – whether or not they are part of an official system. Views and explanations can be put across successfully in briefing groups by word of mouth; facts and figures need a permanent record.

One to many – the speech

Mention company speechmaking and most of our minds flick back to old Anderson waffling on at his retirement thrash, or the Mayor of Blimpton forcing himself to tell a dubious joke at the annual sales conference. Yet these are merely embarrassing apologies for one of the strongest and oldest methods of communication – good old-fashioned oratory.

Words carefully constructed into the memorable phrases of a great speech live in the memory. Pericles at Athens, Lincoln at Gettysburg and Churchill in World War II had no need for briefing group notes or visual aids. The essential information ('Athens is great', 'Democracy rules', 'We will never surrender') was communicated and remembered.

Yet many shy away from public speaking because it takes time and care and practice to do it well – and that is the only way to do it. Manuals have been written on the subject but here is the briefest checklist.

▷ **Analyse your audience.**
▷ **Research your subject.**
▷ **Practise your delivery.**
▷ **Use the minimum of notes.**
▷ **Structure your speech into:**

Introduction;
Statement of purpose;
Body;
Close.
▷ **Keep it simple.**

And, lastly,

▷ **Triple underline your main message with the old formula:**
★ **Tell them what you're going to tell them,**
★ **Tell them, and then**
★ **Tell them what you've told them.**

Talk among yourselves

In the three face-to-face methods we've already scanned, the information is essentially being passed down the line or across the table. True, there will be opportunity for questions, but these will usually arise directly out of the content of the initial message. Control of the message, particularly in the speech, lies with the communicating manager, and the more the message veers towards the *expedient* category, the more control will the speaker wish to exert over the meeting.

But there is, of course, a traditional face-to-face method in which all those present can have a part to play in exchanging information and opinion about the company – the meeting is perhaps the best way of describing it, although it is a meeting in which the aim is to encourage channels of communication from all those present and not simply to expect them to respond to one main channel from the top or from one side or the other.

In public life these meetings range from the monthly gathering of the town or city council to the larger daily talking shops of Westminster or Brussels or Washington. In corporate life they take on the name of Departmental Meeting, Joint Consultative Council, Works Council, Participation Committee, Quality Circle or – yes of course – Board Meeting.

Now essentially these are not in the same category as briefing groups where the sole purpose is to pass on one or more messages and encourage feedback. (Not that many meetings don't stray into this area and develop into an echo chamber for his master's voice, whether his master is chairman, chief executive officer or long-serving shop steward.)
chairman, chief executive officer or long-serving shop steward.)

Yet meetings in which a group of people are each trying to communicate either their own pieces of information or information representing a particular group take up a large quota of corporate time. And it is, I believe, these face-to-face confrontations, and not briefing groups or speeches or personal interviews, that produce, in public as in corporate life, the most hostility, the most misunderstanding, the most dissatisfaction.

John Cleese's training video *Meetings, Bloody Meetings* has passed into corporate folklore, not because of its risqué title, but because it embodies what so many managers feel about the whole interminable process.

And yet to be at a meeting where new facts emerge, where new insights are gained, where each participant strikes sparks of enthusiasm off someone else, and where real progress is made towards achieving agreed objectives, is to see face-to-face communication at its best.

How, then, to make meetings participative and useful? Yes, of course, watch the John Cleese video and go on courses and read more books. But learning what such meetings are about in the head will not alter their effectiveness in our company unless *we* determine to change our attitude towards them. How?

▷ First, the chairman/woman/person must be just that. A facilitator. Someone who directs the ebb and flow of discussion, ensures that everyone has a chance to speak, encourages the reticent, keeps to the agenda, calls a halt – and even reprimands when necessary – but does not dominate, bites their tongue hard when tempted to give their own views – and sticks to time.

▷ Second, the subjects under discussion must be given a time schedule appropriate to their importance. If every company division is allowed to give a full verbal report at the sales conference which could just as easily be committed to paper and circulated beforehand, there will be little time at the end to draw out the crucial reactions to the new product line or the review of competitors' strategy. There must be an appropriate structure within which the meeting can function.

▷ Third, everyone who takes part – and that includes you and me – must be prepared to *listen* to what other people are saying before responding.

Sperry ran an immensely well publicised corporate campaign in the States and later in Europe, based on that very word 'listening'. 'We understand how important it is to listen' was' the tagline which went around the world. Sperry became the 'listening company': the slogan appeared in their press advertisements; it permeated their industrial relations; every employee was committed to a one-day listening seminar; it was a whole new way of life. They taught their managers how to listen first and speak afterwards – and it worked.

The training had four objectives.

▷ **To build an awareness of the importance to business of listening.**
▷ **To increase understanding of the nature of listening and its impact on the total communication process.**
▷ **To diagnose listening abilities and practices.**
▷ **To develop skills and techniques to improve listening effectiveness.**

Stop, look and listen before you condemn those bloody meetings out of hand; they have an important part to play in the communication process.

Consider the amount of information which goes from your company communicators to your corporate audiences on the voice circuit alone. The large total

will include many connections we have not mentioned: the chairman's chat to the merchant banker,
the television interview with the finance director, the
public relations manager's telephone call to the *Financial Times*, the receptionist's reply to the aggrieved
customer, the hint in the washroom, the word to the
lobbyist, the grapevine ...

Planned or unplanned, in isolation or as part of a
concerted force, the power of face-to-face speech
should never be underestimated. It must be controlled
and used skilfully to carry both expected and expedient messages.

Sometimes spoken words are sufficient and can stand alone,
but very often they need reinforcement by the subject of our
next chapter – marks on paper.

7
Marks on paper

Cutting the company cake

IT WAS ANNUAL REPORT time again. The corporate communication department turned over the much-corrected leaves of
previous years' reports, reviewed what BP, IBM and Shell had
done this year and flicked through the list of group products.
What should be sliced and quartered to convey the growth of
the tax bill and the slimness of the profit this year? A pile of
coins, a packing case, a factory silhouette? What about an
actual pound note? Well, no, because the Bank of England was
a bit stuffy about reproduction of its hallowed design and the
Chairman might not like it ... but a *toy* pound note? Perfect. A
nice bright colour. A convenient £100 in bold type which
would divide easily into the appropriate percentages.

The report was in page proof before someone took a
magnifying glass to the design and picked out the single word
MONOPOLY. As the company in question had been the
subject of a recent investigation by the Monopolies Commission it didn't seem the happiest of choices. A more suitable
sacrificial object was found for slicing.

☆   ☆   ☆

IT IS THIS very *permanency* of print which makes it at once so
valuable and yet so fraught with potential error for the
communicating corporation. This is an essential group of
media, yet one to be handled with great care and skill if it is to
be effective. Spoken words will often be forgotten, images will
pass away, but the written word is there for the lifetime of the
paper it is printed on. How can it be used to maximum effect?

Slogans – getting down to basics

The slogan is the simplest expression of the company as communicator: a handful of words and possibly a picture on paper ranging from a single side of A4 to a 48 sheet poster. It will be used almost exclusively externally for promoting your company's *expedient* messages: what you want the public to think of you and your products or services. The sustained creativity of generations of advertising copywriters has produced classics of communication which live on – sometimes even when the product or company itself has disappeared, although the subjects of 'Guinness is good for you', 'You can be sure of Shell', and 'Aah, Bisto!' are, thankfully, still with us, setting a standard of excellence against which to measure 'Pure genius', 'The world's favourite airline' and 'Vorsprung durch Technik'.

But the slogan can also be used to communicate with employee audiences through office and factory posters, often associated with health and safety and dealing with enforced messages. The problems of display and monitoring often reduce the effectiveness of this medium in-company but when it is used effectively, as it was in wartime factories with slogans such as 'Walls have ears' and 'Careless talk costs lives', the results can be memorable.

The slogan secret is to catch a phrase which enforces a reaction from the selected audience, whether they are car drivers passing a poster site at rush hour or patients sitting on the other side of the doctor's waiting room.

Many companies have found it useful to link their corporate name with a slogan on their letterhead, vehicle livery and publications, such as Midland's 'The listening bank' or Philips'

'Simply years ahead'. As part of a total corporate communication campaign this can be of great help in transmitting a long-term message of information or assurance.

Bulletins – the salient facts

As one or two sheets of typewritten or printed paper boldly headed with the company name or logo, the bulletin appears in corporate life in a variety of permutations: as an inter-office memo, as a press release, as an announcement for the notice-board, as an information sheet, as a position paper. But whatever it is called it has the same basic objective, conveying a limited amount of information to a specific audience in the shortest possible time.

The audiences who read bulletins are almost always in a hurry.

The journalist needs to pick out the salient facts and judge whether the information is worth bothering about in the split second it takes to pass before his eyes from the pile on the desk to the pile in the wastebin. 'Do your releases make good pulp?' ran the headline in a communication trade weekly. Most of them from business and industry do: one editor estimates that 95% of releases received go straight into the bin.

The employee needs to gather information in the time it takes to sweep a cursory glance across the bulletin board on the way past to canteen or lunchtime shopping trip.

The financial analyst needs to assimilate facts and figures quickly from your position paper on transatlantic trading to compare with the many other sources gathered on your company before making the monthly report.

The bulletin must be easy to read, simple (but not simplistic) and carefully constructed.

Who better to call on for advice on how to write it than that scourge of Civil Service circumlocutions, Sir Ernest Gowers. He said:

> *'Use no more words than are necessary to express your meaning, for if you use more you are likely to obscure it and to tire your reader. In particular do not use superfluous adjectives and adverbs, and do not use roundabout phrases where single words would serve.'*

He further advised:

> *'Use familiar words rather than the far-fetched, if they express your meaning equally well; for the familiar are more likely to be readily understood.'*

And finally:

> *'Use words with a precise meaning rather than those that are vague, for they will obviously serve better to make your meaning clear; and in particular, prefer concrete words to abstract, for they are more likely to have a precise meaning.'*

This is sound commonsense and any manager would do well to absorb either Gowers' *Plain Words* or the transatlantic equivalent, Strunk and White's *The Elements of Style*, before they write another memo.

However, don't be *too* concise. A decade ago The British Council sent a bulletin to their pensioners with the regular company payment. It read:

'IMPORTANT – if the envelope contains money, check the amount before opening. Claims for shortage will not be considered if the staple or flap has been disturbed.'

Those expecting here some differentiation between the press release and the pay envelope stuffer will be disappointed. I am suggesting that in *all* these cases what you *call* the piece of paper is unimportant. What *is* vitally important is the need and expectation of the audience; and in every case that audience will want the essential facts, clearly set-out and crisply written with all unnecessary verbiage pruned away. Winston Churchill's wartime request for a summary on one side of a sheet of paper was as appropriate for him as it is for us, for the company is always at war – with time, with unresponsiveness, with ignorance and with misunderstanding – and clear, uncomplicated language is a powerful weapon.

Newsletters – information for target groups

As we progress from bulletin to newsletter so the *number* of words increases as well as the diversity of items and potential number of messages that can be communicated.

However, it would be wrong to suggest that an increase in words means an increase in the number of audience groups. The power of the newsletter (and if you need a definition, that currently given by the British Association of Industrial Editors is 'not more than eight pages'), is that it is a regular digest of information, that its readers – because of its format – will not expect sophisticated presentation, and that it is aimed at a specific target group.

Within a company, individual offices, areas, depots and factories may need their own regular newsletters as may specialist function groups such as Research and Development, Finance, Computing and Quality Control.

For outside audiences the newsletter can carry information to shareholders, a local community, institutional investors, dealers, schoolchildren, agencies ...

The strength of the newsletter is that, within its limited format, it can carry pictures and text of variable quality and need not look expensive. Indeed, if the company is concerned about promoting a thrifty image, the newsletter will be an ideal communication medium.

The potential of this format has been better realised in the United States where newsletters on every conceivable topic are not only printed but sold on subscription. In the UK the excellent *Economist* specialist newsletters on trade and telecommunications have shown what can be done; the broking houses, too, have adopted this method for passing out current, detailed information, quickly and in readable format.

Newspapers – telling it like it is

Although the newspaper has lost a little of its credibility since the onward march of television as the People's Communicator, the proliferation of the gutter tabloids and the harsh words and tarnished images of Wapping, it is still one of the bedrock means for corporate communication. Indeed, some public relations companies wrongly assume that the worth of their activity on behalf of a company can still be measured in the sheer monthly footage of newspaper cuttings they secure.

The power of the newspaper lies in its concentration of messages, in its universality of readership and in its speed of recognition and feedback. It is possible for a commentary on your company's half-year figures announced at noon on Wednesday to have been seen and registered by every leading figure in the financial world in the next morning's *Financial Times* or *Wall Street Journal* and for the share price to take a corresponding rise or fall.

It is possible for 14,000 families in Scunthorpe to be aware of your company's proposal to build a small engineering plant there by the Saturday morning following the publication of the *Scunthorpe Star* on Friday.

It is possible for your entire workforce to read details of the company's voluntary redundancy scheme and compare the opinions of unions, management and individual employees in your in-house newspaper three days after the decisive board meeting.

Yes, of course, we all know cases where the possible did not happen, but in the main the newspaper still holds the pre-eminent position if you want to get detailed, illustrated, *printed* information to a large number of people quickly.

Having said this, it is not an easy medium for a company to handle – at any level. Far too many senior executives assume that there is a simple procedure for 'getting it in the paper'. It all depends, we are told, on 'knowing the right chap at the other end'. No, it doesn't happen like that. And as for employees, well it all depends on writing a few stories and dressing up the pages with bold headlines and calling it *Whatsisname's News*. No, it doesn't happen like that either.

Newspaper writing and production, however simple it may appear, is a complex and skilled business, whether at national, local or in-house level. Because readers have always paid far less than they should have done for their 16 pages of newsprint, the medium has in some ways been devalued but, providing one accepts its demands, it can still carry the corporation's messages forcefully and quickly to very many of its audiences. And, please note, it is *not* an audience itself: the corporate communicator does not develop press relations for the sake of the Press but for what can be communicated *through* the Press to particular audiences. In other words, do not be impressed by the quantity of press releases issued by your company or its consultants, but by the *effect* of those releases.

Magazines – the leisurely influence

If the newspaper is the delivery van in message-carrying then the magazine is the limousine. Sleeker, softer, a more leisurely ride – even though there's often a hidden punch in the engine.

Although a number of 'news magazines' straddle the field between the two media, the magazine is not simply – indeed, not primarily – a medium dependent on its format. Inside British and American businesses are many so-called 'company newspapers', for example, which are in reality magazines. Their stories, their frequency, their whole approach to the business of communication, is slow and leisurely and non-dateable. On the other hand such 'magazines' as the *Economist*, *Newsweek* and *Time International* are really 'newspapers' in their fast response to current news, their up-to-date commentaries and their fadeability.

The labelling of these publications is in the eyes of the readers and in their approach to the marks on the paper before them. The magazine, with its higher standards of production, its improved physical feel, its potential for good illustration and colour, its opportunity for advanced typography and artwork, is the right medium for the company's messages in greater length and detail; and is perhaps the most assured way of establishing a long-term reference to those corporate policies, activities and achievements at the centre of our information complex.

While newspapers are *generalist* in their approach, magazines are in the main *specialist* (and I include in that definition most of the trade journals which now appear in a newspaper format). In that specialism lies an excellent opportunity to get your company messages across to such diverse groups as conservationists, local councillors, administration managers, owners of expensive houses, small investors, economists, architects ... the list is endless.

On the employee front the magazine was once the *only* form of regular printed communication, but the newly-found ability to run a few thousand copies of a newspaper on a colour web-offset press and the growing demand for faster information in a recognisable format has meant that newspapers now lead magazines by about two to one.

This does not mean, as I've said, that a change of format is always successful; indeed, house journalism is littered with pseudo newspapers printed on glossy paper and lacking any important current news items. These are simply magazines in tabloid clothing. But the general house magazine, with a smattering of current news and a bulk of feature articles and colour pictures, is still very much alive and a useful and trusted communication method for many corporations.

Reports – bare facts about the company

So important has the concept of the company annual report and accounts become in corporate communication that some specialist agencies produce and advise on nothing else. This is the public face of the company in print, this is what is handed to the casual enquirer at the front office, sent to the shareholder, scanned by the prospective graduate job hunter, dissected by the City editor and the financial analyst.

The report is often the jewel in the corporate literature crown, yet too often it has been hamstrung in its effectiveness by turgid, lengthy epistles from the chairman and managing director, minute colour portraits of the entire board of directors, and densely packed columns of statutory accounts. The predominant attitude has been to treat it like a dose of cough medicine: 'It's going to be nasty – so let's get rid of it as quickly as possible.'

The efforts of competitions and specialist report writers and designers on both sides of the Atlantic are now swinging the pendulum the other way so that it is sometimes difficult to distinguish the annual report from an art gallery catalogue bound into a set of tax tables.

A little common sense needs to be applied to the use of this medium so that we can put its potential into perspective. Look at your own report and ask:

▷ Does it state the aims of the organisation?

▷ Does it have objectives and does it meet them by making appropriate points?

▷ Is it graphically pleasing?

▷ Does the cover make you want to read it – will it get noticed?

▷ Can you sum up in five words the main impression the report is trying to make?

▷ Does it look too cheap – or too expensive?

▷ Does it make the company seem different from other companies?

▷ Does it rapidly convey what business(es) the company is in?

▷ Does it meet the regulations?

▷ Is it readable?

▷ Has the company made a special effort to make the financial pages clear and appealing?

For many years most companies concentrated on getting across their annual financial message in the report and accounts to their shareholders and the City. In recent years it has been on the employee report, the 'pop' accounts, that the bright lights of advisers and designers have shone. For some companies this simplified version has turned out to be the perfect medium for informing not only its employees but its shareholders as well, who often prefer the scaled-down, pictorial edition to the original official version.

Like their fatter brothers, employee reports now have their own competitions and awards and their own predictable formats; such as putting the fruits of employee labours into acceptable, socially-relevant conversions, such as,

---

Did you know that the profit from your efforts in this financial year was enough to staff ten hospitals and run five fire stations for three months?

As with annual reports and accounts before them, the employee versions are too often concerned with producing elaborate pictorial and wordy variations on the financial theme (coins, biscuits, bottles of squash and pizzas, all sliced into meaningful segments). What employees actually *want* to read is often a more basic, simple appraisal of where the company is, where it is going and what that means for them.

The Industrial Society has taken a prominent part in promoting better employee reporting in recent years. It recommends that employees need to understand the *meaning* of financial information and the terms used; the *significance* of the figures themselves and the *impact* of the message. In the printed report itself, the IS looks for:

 ▷ good visual impact and design;
 ▷ a clear explanation of the current financial position and performance;
 ▷ translation of financial jargon into plain, under-standable English;

▷ a description of the business and its corporate structure;

▷ an assessment of plans, future objectives and prospects.

And that, come to think of it, is a sound basis for the full-blown annual report and accounts itself. In fact, moves have been made to combine a simplified report for all audiences with a hard batch of the statutory figures on plain paper to satisfy the financial experts. It's an uneasy blend of the *enforced*, the *expected* and the *expedient* and so far there have been few successes.

Leaflets – the direct alternative

When the British Government decided to launch an information campaign about the facts and fallacies of AIDS it used a double-headed media programme to communicate with the country-wide audience: a television commercial and a leaflet.

It may be thought that in this electronic age the words and pictures on the small screen were the preferred way of communicating this vital information – but not so.

When criticised for the lack of detail in the television commercial the Department of Health spokesman replied that providing information was not its purpose. Its purpose was to get people to read the leaflet, the real information carrier.

The order of priority was made possible because of the immense growth in recent years in leaflet distribution, both through the post office and independent direct mail organisations. It was possible for 23 million copies of the slim AIDS leaflet to be dropped through the letterboxes of the land.

Like the bulletin, the leaflet is essentially a communicator of hard facts, but here the austere bleakness of the bulletin is replaced by typeset copy, design, illustration and often colour printing. Its purpose is to provide information which may well be kept and reread and it slots into the company communication programme in many ways: internally providing facts on pension schemes, safety procedures, mission statements and job induction; externally on service and product specification, position statements, savings and investment schemes for banks and descriptions of herbs and meat and tropical fruit for supermarkets. A jack of all trades.

Brochures – the glossy image

The word 'glossy' has almost become synonymous with the word 'brochure'. By this title even the heaviest, wordiest slab of print has acquired an almost derogatory air; a hint of the sharp salesman, a touch of shine without substance.

Yet brochures and catalogues, although among the most costly media to produce, with their full-colour printing and expensive photography, have a solidity which makes them an ideal carrier of expedient messages.

Strangely enough, they can operate at two ends of a sliding scale with equal effectiveness. As the ultimate coffee table publication they can exude a sense of wealth, knowledge and excellence which, although perhaps more suitable for the fifties and sixties than the leaner times in which we live, can still carry a particular message to existing and potential customers like no other medium.

At the other end of the scale consider the way in which brochures have become the annual key to business for the travel agencies and seed merchants, have turned themselves into bookstall revenue earners for Habitat, Harrods, Selfridges and Laura Ashley, and have become the raison d'être for business itself for Argos, Littlewoods and Freemans.

As in every case, the medium must be weighed against the needs of the audience; and there *is* an audience who, when the subject matter is attractive enough, will sit down and leaf through a hundred pages or more at a sitting and enjoy the experience.

Books – a limited appeal

It would be wrong to close this section without mentioning the medium you are in the process of reading: the printed book. It's not often thought of as an effective weapon in the corporate communication armoury: it's slow to impart information, it's ponderous, it's relatively expensive to produce and it has a long gestation period.

But the book has its uses: as a record of company history, as the celebration of fifty, a hundred, two hundred years of corporate effort, as the definition of a trade, industry or profession – *The Story of Wool, H J Heinz, The History of ICI, The Romance of Coal*. Such books, almost always printed privately or sponsored, have a part to play in reinforcing a corporate name among shareholders, employees and the general public and can also play an effective educative role in schools and universities.

Moods of expectation

This procession of types of printed material may have seemed too obvious to you. Of course you know there are magazines and newspapers and bulletins and posters and books. You read them every day; they are part of all our lives.

But when you read them you read them in a different mood of expectation for each medium – that is the point. And I believe companies are too often in such a hurry to communicate a message that they confuse the media and choose the wrong one.

Each of the media we have been looking at is essentially a mixture of words or words and pictures, dressed up in a particular format with which we have become familiar over long use. The amount of time the reader has to give to each of the formats, the kind of information we want to put across, the speed with which we wish to do it and the chances of its being read and understood by the greatest number of our target audiences must all be considered before we begin to write or to commission others to write. What shall it be?

A slogan?	**A magazine?**
A bulletin?	**A leaflet?**
A newsletter?	**A brochure?**
A newspaper?	**A book?**

Perhaps a combination of two or more printed media should be used to ensure that the messages are received. Perhaps also, just as we often need to combine one of the spoken media with one from the print selection, so we shall need to support or supplement our words on paper with words on tape and pictures on film. That is the topic for our next chapter.

8
Sound and vision

Projecting the right image

THE CONFERENCE AUDITORIUM was full of researchers and scientists – as well as a sprinkling of senior company executives. The atmosphere was earnest, restrained, and more than a little dull. There had been presentations in which complex diagrams, detailed numerical tables and enlargements from the electron microscope had filled the screen to an awed hush.

Then the company's new development director took the rostrum and pressed the remote-control button. Up on the screen flashed three slides in quick succession: Marilyn Monroe, The Pope and Her Majesty the Queen. A noticeable buzz of comment ran through the audience.

'I'm not going to talk about any of them,' said the speaker. 'That was just to get your attention.' It did.

IN COMPLETING our review of corporate communication media we now move into a third group which must be given as much consideration as speech or print even though they are still viewed by some managers with all the enthusiasm of a Luddite for a spinning jenny. Yes, these are the media which need some kind of mechanical apparatus, either electric or electronic, for their operation. Elements of speech and print still have a place in these newer systems; it is simply that they are being projected to our audiences in a new dimension.

Audio – his master's voice

Take speech. To move the briefing talk one stage further and record it is a natural progression. Even the now dating long-playing plastic disc helped a major electronics company to tell its story to potential graduate employees in an audible corporate review. There is still a demand, especially in North America, for flexible plastic message discs which can be sent through the post or included in magazines to tell customers about new products, give Christmas greetings to employees or simply play a selection of advertising jingles. However, such activity is limited compared to the use and potential of the audio tape.

Once a master tape has been made under studio conditions, such tapes can be mass-produced in their hundreds at low cost. Their uses are legion. One pharmaceutical group found that it had a problem updating its salesmen with technical details of new products. They were busy people, always on the road. By fitting a cassette player in each car and providing a monthly product update tape, the salesman could increase his knowledge between calls and then replay to check that he had all the facts before the next appointment.

To keep staff up to date with company news, BOC prepare a daily news tape which is placed in an answering machine by noon each day so that any employee can dial the number and listen in.

The British Institute of Management's *Management Tape* gives subscribers to the scheme an hour of news and features on management topics which can then be passed to other members of the same company or held in the library for reference.

If companies use this method instead of the more usual newsletter for communicating with senior management, it holds the added advantage of being much less easy to leak if confidential information is included.

Most major conferences now have on-site recording units so that speeches and debates can be purchased to take home or be sent on within a few days. Specially prepared news and feature items on a particular company event or product can be distributed to local radio stations with often a better chance of being used than a traditional press release.

As with all other media discussed in this section, the audio tape, simple as it may sound, is not easy to produce: expertise and equipment will have to be invested, either in-house or outside, before this method can achieve its high potential.

Slide/sound – help or hindrance?

The projection of a slide on a screen has long been part of corporate life; the wonder is that even after years of use the plaintive cry still goes up from the floor of the darkened ballroom: 'Er ... we seem to have got that the wrong way round. Oh well, let's go on to the next one.'

The use of the slide, whether on an overhead or on a 35 millimetre projector, has traditionally been for speaker support, although many of those who are masters of that one-to-many technique rely solely – and often most successfully – on the voice.

The mechanical techniques must be mastered. That is not our concern here – there are many textbooks and courses on the subject – but in evaluating it as a *communication* medium, the criteria applied to any back-up illustration on the screen should be:

▷ **Does it assist communication?**
▷ **Is it absolutely necessary?**
▷ **Does it provide** *additional* **information which cannot be spoken?**
▷ **Does it enhance the spoken word and not confuse it?**

Because the OHP and the slide projector are so often used it's assumed that anyone can prepare the slides. Not so. Far too many presentations are ruined by illegible or minute writing or typing, forgettable and amateur photography and, worst of all, by an exact duplicate of the speaker's words going on the screen as he or she speaks in (almost) complete synchronisation.

But the use of the projected image goes much further than the speaker's aid. A set of slides with a pulsed tape commentary has a great range of uses: as an induction package; sent to remote company branches as a substitute for a central meeting; as a discussion starter for briefing groups; as an introductory ten minutes for a company speaker touring community associations with a company message; as part of an exhibition stand. The latest all-in-one magic boxes combining screen, tape and slide carousel have many uses in and out of company.

The outstanding advantage of this type of communication package is both the potential high clarity of 35mm slides themselves and their interchangeability to make way for updated figures or two or three local shots to personalise the presentation. Today the scope of the slide has been immeasurably increased by the development of several systems of computer graphics origination equipment which can mix and match a kaleidoscope of charts, drawings, computer-art, still and live film and actual three-dimensional objects onto one slide.

At its most ambitious, the humble slide can feature in a battery of twenty, thirty or forty projectors and dissolve units to provide a highly dramatic presentation eminently suitable for product launches, sales conferences and association conventions and exhibitions. At this level the medium is in direct competition, for price and effectiveness, with the video film.

Moving pictures – the main attraction?

The mass-projector spectacular moves close to the motion picture without capturing its essential communication quality – movement of the image with synchronised sound. We may discuss 16mm film or video or television and the many and varied ways these can be combined and elaborated, but essentially – so far as the method of communication is concerned – it is getting a moving image in front of the target audience with accompanying sound. That can be done on a whitewashed wall in a village institute or on the glass-fronted boxes in more than 20 million homes in the UK alone.

The corporation has always been keen to use the moving picture. In the forties, fifties and sixties the film libraries of multinationals such as Shell and BP carried the work of some of the best documentary directors in the business. As well as aiming at the traditional audiences in education and local communities, it was not unknown for some of the cinema chains to show the occasional company epic.

Some of those films are still available today – on video cassette to cater for the new audiences who have been weaned over to the small screen.

Television itself has become of prime use to the company in communicating with potential customers and it is with the advertising commercial that television has come to dominate external communication budgets, often linked to the repetition of the campaign theme in print through press advertisements and posters, and in audio on commercial radio.

But television also provides the opportunity for the company to present itself through its top or specialist executives on news interviews, business and science programmes, debates, special features and, not always so happily, investigations. The same can also be said of radio and, just as the main political parties have invested heavily in television-training for their key speakers, so television and radio training has become part of many larger companies' communication strategies. Indeed, the choice of who is to be the spokesman during a period of company newsworthiness, may depend not on seniority or knowledge but on being able to put an acceptable face on the box. This was conclusively demonstrated during the 1984–5 coal strike when Michael Eaton took over as National Coal Board spokesman to dilute the implacable image projected by Chairman Ian MacGregor.

Commercial television can also be used deliberately by companies to speak to selected audiences. In the mid '70s Trust House Forte took three minutes at noon one Sunday to speak to all their employees across the country: an exercise which also depended, of course, on using print and word of mouth to ensure that the employees were watching the box at the right time!

News on the pipeline

But it has been the video cassette that has attracted so many companies to the moving image department in recent years. Back in 1981 National Westminster stepped into private television with a 1,000 machine network and an initial budget of over £2m with which to improve its employee communication system. Many other larger companies, particularly banks and insurance firms, have followed its example. With small pockets of staff scattered throughout the country, the video cassette seemed the ideal way of communicating development news and details of services and schemes. Nat West's involvement has been maintained; it now uses a network of 2,550 machines to screen productions in both U-matic and VHS formats. BP is also a great video user and its regular in-company news programme *Pipeline*, with the eloquent Brian Redhead up front, has been winning awards since the first pot-pourri of business stories went up on monitors all over the BP world in 1978.

And video has its external uses. During the successful bid for Debenhams by the Burton Group in 1986, 4,500 copies of a specially made video were requested by Debenhams' shareholders. Burton's Publicity Director, Richard Birtchnell, said:

> *There is no doubt it helped us win the takeover ... Corporate video in this form made history.*

Specific research backed up the Burton statement but in many cases of mass use of video the vital questions have not been asked. A questionnaire put to major users of in-company videos as late as 1984 came to the sad conclusion that although companies may be willing to spend heavily on the medium they had little idea whether it was working.

But accepting this, and forgetting the tens of thousands of pounds worth of video hardware that has been left to gather dust in company storage cupboards, the impact of video on industry and its general acceptance as a communication medium is now certain. What still has to be done is to use it effectively and monitor its effects.

Electronics – the voice of the future

Industry has been talking about the Great Information Technology Revolution for a decade. Remember Britain's Information Technology Year? Every manager a terminal case? Well, it hasn't happened. The natural reluctance of managers to get involved with anything more technical than an office stapler has slowed down the potential growth of the new electronic communications hardware as surely as it did with the carousel slide projector. But in this case the gospel is taking rather longer to be accepted because the electronic media require *personal* involvement for maximum effect. The naturally reticent British manager is here falling behind his American and European colleagues in having the necessary confidence to grapple with the teleconferencing facility on the new composite phone system, or to plug in to the company news database on the computer network, or to word process his own reports while commuting to Basingstoke.

Nevertheless, electronic media *must* be included in any potential corporate communication policy. It does, as the Digital Equipment Company has discovered, add a new dimension.

Digital employs nearly 90,000 staff in some 660 sales, service, manufacturing and engineering locations in 48 countries and as Anne Kreidler, manager of corporate employee communication, explained:

> '*There was just no way to reach them quickly should a critical issue come up.*'

Now the first steps have been taken to implement *Live Wire*, claimed by Digital as 'the first fully-distributed electronic bulletin board in existence'. Using networks of compatible equipment, (Digital, of course), the system enables the company to communicate almost instantaneously with its thousands of employees throughout the world.

This paperless communication system reaches the majority of employees through their individual computer terminals; the rest have access to the bulletins through public terminals in reception areas, cafeterias and lounges.

Sponsorship – the intangible approach

At the end of this section of new dimensions for communication media, comes one which may seem slightly out of place: sponsorship. This is not talk or print or recorded sound or moving pictures, although all these may have some part in how it is eventually made visible. Neither is it a way of conveying enforced or expected messages. It certainly shows the company in an expedient 'look at me' mode, but sometimes the chances of any real benefit for the company are remote and altruism begins to show a surprised but grateful face in company affairs.

It could be argued that just as there is no such thing as a free lunch, so there is no sponsorship which does not reflect well on the sponsor. That has almost been proved incorrect. How many knew more about Cornhill Insurance after their last sponsored Test Match than before they started? Did Schweppes *really* sell more soft drinks by spending a million pounds on linking their name with the UK County Cricket Championship? When the curtain comes down on a performance at the Royal Opera House on a particular evening do x per cent of the audience switch their current accounts to Midland Bank?

Those companies who specialise in company sponsorship would suggest that such a crude link between increased business and sponsorship is irrational and that the real benefits, the actual messages conveyed, are almost subliminal in their effect. And in any case the avowed objective of many sponsorships is not to convey a distinct message to the public but to transfer a number of lower-key expedient messages to small groups of dealers, customers and employees who are involved on an entertainment basis.

But whatever your views on sponsorship, the medium must be considered as one of the choices available for the company communication programme, although to pinpoint the messages it should carry may be rather more difficult.

By adopting again the concept of the overall method rather than the more usually accepted form of the specific item, we can add five more main types of media to those already discussed.

AUDIO – cassettes for convenient, instant and confidential communication.

SLIDE/SOUND – not only speaker support but also compact, flexible programmes.

MOVING PICTURES – the timeless attraction of film, on large and small screen.

ELECTRONIC – computer-generated information before your eyes.

SPONSORSHIP – the subliminal factor.

Having progressed from the company and its communicators to those they communicate with, what there is to say and how they can say it, we are able to range the audiences on one side, the messages on another, the media on a third – and make our choices. Such a manoeuvre takes time, care, skill ... and another chapter.

9
Communication in action

Crisis in microcosm

THE 1980s have been littered with companies forced into difficult communication situations and finding themselves unprepared and ill-equipped to meet the demands being made on them by the many audiences outside their tightly patrolled boundaries. I don't just mean deregulation in the City of London or Chernobyl or Bhopal or Tylenol but any situation in a company's life which leaves it without the necessary message to communicate – enforced, expected or expedient.

The larger moments of unpreparedness have been given a separate slot in the communication phrasebook: they're now called

CRISIS COMMUNICATION

and they have their own specialist gurus. But any situation which leaves the company with its mouth open but speechless when a message should be given is the same: crisis communication in microcosm.

In the experienced words of Harvey Thomas, the Conservative Party's director of press and communications:

> 'I can make sure the slide is in focus, I can make sure that there's a good white screen, I can make sure the lights are turned off in the auditorium, I can make sure the sound synch is connected. The one thing I cannot do is project a slide that isn't in the projector.'

For many companies there never is the right slide in the

projector because it hasn't been thought necessary or considered or planned – there has been no corporate communication strategy. However, now that we have looked at the audiences, the messages and the means of communication, we are able to construct the scaffolding within which to build one: a three-way matrix which will enable us to place any particular message for any specific audience within the context of a suitable selection of media. We might visualise it like a pyramid.

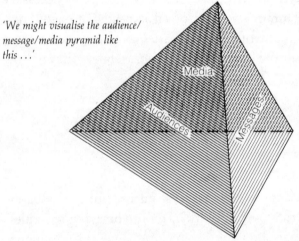

*'We might visualise the audience/
message/media pyramid like
this ...'*

Using an audiences/messages media pyramid we can select typical situations in corporate life and see how different companies have channelled specific messages to selected audiences.

Salvaging disaster – the CIA after Bhopal

Britain's chemicals industry will live with the 'spectre of

Bhopal', in the form of media references to the Indian disaster, for years to come.

Before the leak of poisonous gas on 3 December 1984, the Chemical Industries Association in the UK was already planning a major campaign to raise public awareness of its members' value to society after a poll result which showed that only 29 per cent of the general public had a favourable view of chemical manufacturers, compared with 50 per cent five years earlier.

After Bhopal, even the most cynical of CIA members no longer doubted the justification for an intensive community relations campaign. Community information publications and exhibition stands tackled issues such as concern over plant safety and road transport hazards head-on and are now in extensive use by companies whose previous policy had been low-profile on neighbourhood publicity.

Some 300,000 copies of booklets and broadsheets were distributed, backed up by packs to help inexperienced public speakers put their message across to community organisations.

More than 100 CIA member companies have shown a video, *Chemicals with Care*, to councillors and local opinion-formers. The video was produced within months of the Bhopal disaster.

On a national Chemical Industry Open Day in the autumn of 1986 over 200,000 people living near chemical plants visited production sites to see products and meet employees. Said Philip Dewhurst, Head of Public Relations at the CIA:

'In my view this created a more lasting and cost-effective impression than millions spent on corporate advertising.'

THE MESSAGE (expedient): the UK chemical industry is of immense value to society and, despite
disasters like Bhopal, has an excellent safety record.
THE AUDIENCES (product and Government
related): the general public, local councillors, opinion-
formers and residents in areas surrounding chemical
plants.
THE MEDIA: *Face to face* factory interviews, speeches;
Print leaflets, broadsheets, display stands, briefing
notes;
Sound and vision slides for speaker support, video film.

Defending against takeover – the Booker McConnell solution

In June 1984, The Dee Corporation announced a £232 million
bid for Booker McConnell PLC without any prior consultation
with the company. Booker had attached small importance to
cultivating the financial press and its image was poor in the
investment community. Despite much rationalisation and
restructuring since 1980, the company was still perceived as an
unwieldy conglomerate.

The timing of the bid was excellent, three months after
Booker's year-end announcement and two months before
Dee's year-end figures.

In careful liaison with the merchant bank, Booker's consultants Valin Pollen drew up a programme of research, press
relations, lobbying, organising of information and advertising.

A research study was implemented to give the company a benchmark as to how it was perceived in the City and two further studies were conducted to monitor progress.

Beginning with a press release on the day of the bid, a sustained programme of press relations was launched, which involved the Chairman undertaking a series of press lunches with City editors and leading journalists.

Members of Parliament, civil servants, influential friends of the company, employees and customers were all lobbied in an orchestrated campaign to have the bid referred to the Monopolies and Mergers Commission (MMC). This involved drafting and production of letters and other literature.

The consultants prepared a brochure which was circulated to all shareholders. Entitled *The Booker Profile* it recounted how the company had been rationalised and made clear the potential of the company under its existing management.

A video film was produced for institutional briefings, along with charts for analysts meetings and for the presentation to the MMC.

Under agency guidance, the company instigated a corporate advertising campaign in the period running up to the MMC's report, hammering home the strengths and future potential of Booker McConnell.

Despite vigorous lobbyings from The Dee Corporation, and although perceptions traditionally take a long time to change, the image of Booker McConnell in the City and in the financial press has improved as a result of this action and, equally important, the City audience is more informed.

The result of the programme was that the bid itself was referred to the MMC, allowing the company to prove its potential and double its interim profits.

THE MESSAGE (expedient): Booker McConnell is a structured company with a bright future.

THE AUDIENCES (finance and Government related): financial analysts, institutional investors, shareholders, MPs, Government departments, customers, employees.

THE MEDIA: *face to face* lobbying, briefings;
print letters, briefing papers, charts, brochure, slogans;
sound and vision video film, advertising film.

Financial facts for employees – Cadbury Schweppes' U-turn

The Cadbury Schweppes Group in the UK has a creditable history of employee information and participation. Financial information is regularly relayed through participation meetings at all levels but, in addition to this democratic process, a fail-safe system operates so that individual employees are given basic facts about the company's progress.

This information channel concentrates around the release of the half-year figures in September and, primarily, the publication of the full year figures in April. On the day the results are announced by the Stock Exchange a poster appears with the key figures on all UK site bulletin boards and a release from the Chairman goes to all management, participation representatives and noticeboards. These provide the nub of the financial results: key figures and a brief commentary.

Following this exercise the results and press reaction appear in the divisional tabloid newspapers and are discussed in meetings with the Chairman, supported by a 35mm slide pack, at all main factory sites.

By the time the annual report and accounts appears in the first week of April, the key figures of profit and loss have been repeated several times through company channels – but it would be naive to assume that they have been generally understood.

Against this background the report to employees is issued with an approach which has to be significantly different to the bulkier, and more wordy statutory document.

For some years a colour tabloid newspaper was produced. Although it was called *People* it contained lengthy statements by the Chairman, Chief Executive and UK Managing Director and no sign of people at work. Its original aims grew further away and pick-up rates on sites fell rapidly.

It was easy enough to criticise what had been done before; more difficult to do something better. Drawing on the experience of other companies, it was decided to try to answer specific questions: 'What happened last year?' 'What's going to happen this year?' 'What about the things you haven't told me?' A six-page A4 publication was produced with the essential facts and none of the long-winded trimmings of the past. The publication was even put out in boxes with a welcoming 'Pick up your copy of *CS Report*'.

Alas, no-one recognised this was the new version of the old *People*. The lack of full colour was criticised and the use of a bar of chocolate and a bottle of Schweppes tonic divided into turnover segments proved to be unreadable. When the pick-up boxes were stacked together on larger sites, the sides of the instruction flaps were torn off, leaving the undying phrase 'up your copy'. Questions were raised in the company conference.

Whatever the merits of the two-colour *CS Report*, it had jolted the system into life; it had broken the mould. The internal employee communication department acted as brokers between the top three directors and the Participation Standing Committee to find out what employees actually wanted and re-define the objectives of the publication. An outside specialist company was called in to look at the design and the overall concept.

The focus of the new look was on people at work. In addition, the financial facts were explained in a short glossary. UK sites were shown on a map and company products were included. Commentaries from the top three each covered one particular area and their contributions were edited to length. The title reverted to *People*, pick-up boxes were retained but redesigned and a matching poster advising employees that '*People* is coming' was distributed to all sites two weeks before delivery.

The reaction to the new format was favourable: from all sides came the comment that, at last, the company had got it right. Regular meetings with the participation committee ensured that the following year's report would be further improved despite a general reaction to an internal spot-check survey of 'no change required'.

THE MESSAGE (enforced/expected): the key points in the company's annual report.
THE AUDIENCES (employee related): senior, middle and junior management; blue and white collar staff.
THE MEDIA: *face to face* **briefing groups; Chairman's speeches;**

print employee report *People*; results poster; results bulletin;
sound and vision slide support for speeches.

Improving the business – into tomorrow with ICL

Until 1982, ICL's presence in retail computer systems had been insignificant. In that year, however, ICL adopted a new market strategy that focused on the retail sector as one of six identified growth areas.

By late 1984, the company had made significant inroads in this sector, and had become No 2 in the market, supplying electronic point of sale and computer systems to several major high street retailers. However, because of the company's relatively recent entry to the market and its chequered history following the merger with STC, ICL was not seen by board level retail decision-makers as a 'first choice' supplier.

The public relations agency Paragon Communications was briefed to mount a communication campaign to address the problem.

A research study aimed at retail board directors, independent consultants and journalists, helped define three principal tasks for the campaign:

▷ **To identify ICL as retail market leader, since only 25 per cent of respondents saw ICL in that role.**

129

 ▷ To show that ICL was committed to the retail
   sector.
 ▷ To demonstrate that ICL had a clear long-term
   strategy for the retail sector and a knowledge of its
   future needs.

It was evident that the campaign needed to achieve results
quickly since the market was by then expanding at around 80
per cent a year and ICL was in danger of being left behind. The
agency decided on a strategy that would create massive impact
for ICL, as a leader in retail technology, as early as possible in
the campaign. A planned follow-up programme would then
build upon the openings created.

It was agreed to create the first ever report on the impact of
technology on retailing, and launch it to ensure the widest
possible exposure for ICL as the leader in this market. Follow-
up activities were designed to support ICL's contention for the
market leader role and provide opportunities for face-to-face
communication with retail board directors and consultants.

This report had to be totally authoritative and credible if it
was to have the impact needed on the retail sector. It also had
to contain carefully targeted angles for all the important retail,
business and consumer media if it was to achieve the
widespread coverage needed to deliver all the messages
identified in the research.

The report was entitled *Retailing Tomorrow* and its launch
included:

▷ an advance briefing for 30 top retailers;
▷ a simultaneous mailing to all retail directors in Britain;
▷ a press launch, supported by audio visual, attended by over 60 leading business, retail and consumer media;
▷ a similar, but separate, launch for consultants;
▷ a programme of live media interviews and mailings to 1,500 relevant media throughout the UK.

Further activities building on the results of the report included editors' briefings, speeches at industry events by ICL spokesmen, editorial case histories on ICL's retailer customers, sales force briefings showing ICL staff how to exploit *Retailing Tomorrow* as a sales aid.

As a result of this campaign, tracking research showed a marked increase in perceptions of ICL as a market leader, a supplier committed to retail and one with a clear strategy for the future.

THE MESSAGES (expedient): ICL is a retail market leader, is committed to the retail sector and has a clear long-term strategy and a knowledge of the future needs of the sector.
THE AUDIENCES (product related): retail board directors and sector consultants.
THE MEDIA: *face to face* briefing groups; speeches;

131

interviews with senior journalists and on radio;
print *Retailing Tomorrow* report; invitations; press releases;
sound and vision audio-visual 35mm slide show.

Tapping community concern – Strathclyde helps young offenders

In Scotland, children who commit offences (apart from specific cases) or who may be in need of care and protection, go before a Children's Panel Hearing instead of a Juvenile Court.

Members of these panels are recruited from people over a wide range of occupation, neighbourhood, age and income groups. All have experience of, and interest in, children and the ability to communicate with them and their families. Members are carefully prepared for their talks through initial training programmes.

Now, every year Strathclyde Regional Children's Panel requires up to 100 new panel members, which involves interviewing some 400 applicants. In 1984 the Strathclyde Regional Children's Panel Advisory Committee (CPAC) was told that there would no longer be an advertising campaign funded by the Scottish Information Office and they must make their own arrangements. They turned to the regional council's public relations department for help.

From discussions with the committee and from public awareness research, the department found that public awareness of the Children's Panel and the Hearing system was low and that, in any case, awareness was distorted by the mistaken belief that some qualification was necessary. In fact, the greatest need articulated by the CPAC was for 'working class' people to serve on panels within their own area.

Two areas had to be tackled: making the public more aware of the system and recruiting potential panel members. However, as interviews had to be completed fairly quickly the two-phase campaign had to be encapsulated in one phase, both explaining and promoting the system and attracting potential members.

Survey research had shown that Strathclyde had the highest household ownership of video recorders in Britain; in some areas this exceeded 50 per cent, and often these areas were the very ones where awareness was low and recruitment difficult.

So the thrust of the campaign was developed as a 'video leaflet': taking the CPAC message into the living rooms of the target group.

A general theme was found for the operation: 'Help put back the pieces'; and the video, which 'starred' four real panel members, was given a press conference premiere which gained extensive media coverage.

The video was offered on a free two-week loan, using Freepost, and was backed by a limited advertising campaign in the Strathclyde newspapers. In addition, a specially-designed exhibition bus with video facilities toured the area, there were leaflet drops to selected districts and a community magazine campaign with free inserts.

In the first three weeks of the campaign over 1,200 requests for the video and information were received and such has been the success of the scheme that the public relations department has been commissioned to run a similar recruitment campaign to promote fostering and adoption.

THE MESSAGES (enforced and expedient): how the Children's Panel Hearings work. The need for people to come forward as panel members.

THE AUDIENCES (product related): general public in the Strathclyde area, particularly 'working class' individuals with an interest in children.

THE MEDIA: *face to face* briefing groups, media interviews;

print leaflets, press advertising, magazine inserts, advertising bus;

sound and vision video cassettes.

Blowing the corporate trumpet

In these five cases studies we've seen the company communicators take hold of one or more messages and use selected media to put those messages across to various audiences. Some cases make impressive (and expensive) reading. Others, such as Strathclyde's, are more modest but, in their own way, just as effective.

Please note two significant factors about these cases: they were *co-ordinated* and they all involved *research* of some kind.

It is these two themes which ought to run through any communication programme you are planning to play on the corporate trumpet, now or in the future. We've already looked at the dangers of gearing the company to a purely *re*-active, one-off approach to communication. The antithesis of this – and the only sensible way to make full and proper use of communication in business – is to plan a *co-ordinated* programme so that, over time and using the right media for the job, a succession of messages can be efficiently channelled to those who are entitled, or expecting, or encouraged to hear them.

The importance of using research to find out whether you have communicated at all, and what reaction you are getting, is discussed in the final chapter. What must be stressed now is that, as these case histories show, in the corporate ABC

RESEARCH COMES BEFORE COMMUNICATION

It would be a sobering sight to see the millions of booklets, the miles of video film, the acres of advertising which have been totally wasted by companies who have decided what and how to communicate purely on the thoughts of the chief executive, on a gut reaction from the personnel manager or on an inspired idea from the head of marketing. The thoughts *may* be accurate, the feeling *may* be correct but this approach has more in common with Roman emperors reading forthcoming events in a pigeon's entrails than with modern business practice. Product manufacture would be rightly criticised if it did not include an integrated research element. Communication structure must be equally reliant on carefully-planned and professionally-administered research programmes.

If we refer to the audience/message/media pyramid as the scaffolding within which an effective corporate communication programme can be erected, then solid research must be the foundation on which that programme is built.

'... solid research must be the foundation on which an effective communication programme is built.

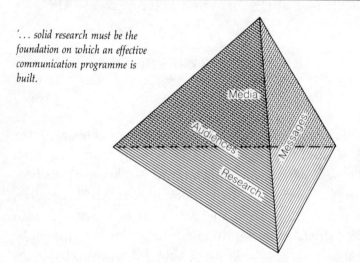

From simple sources we have begun to weave a communication pattern which involves a huge selection of messages, audiences and media, sometimes co-existing and supportive, sometimes conflicting. Who is to identify the audiences, sort and select the messages and choose the media? Who is to direct the individual benefits of each operation into a coherent and effective programme?

This is a question which involves competing claims, professional jealousies, statements of intent, power and money and job descriptions. It's a question to which we'll devote the next chapter.

10
Bring on the specialists

What's in a name?

Edward L Bernays, the veteran American public relations practitioner, answered the question of how his job should be described.

'I don't care what you call me,' he said. 'I know what I do.'

When we ask which specialists are to handle the company's communication needs we immediately find ourselves in an etymological quagmire. The whole area of corporate communication is veiled in a mist of confusion as to name and function.

Public relations, public affairs, marketing, communications manager, PRO, crisis communication, corporate affairs, advertising agency, one-stop house, publicity manager ... this sea of names washes through the pages of the trade journals and on to the desk of the company manager through the financial and management press and in agency brochures and presentation videos.

It would be foolhardy to expect an agreed definition of terms and titles. Nevertheless, it *is* important for company communicators to have a general grasp of what these terms *may* mean to different people. Let's scan the signboards outside the many specialist encampments to find a general definition of what each of them offers.

PUBLIC RELATIONS

Perhaps the most difficult term to define: even those who call themselves public relations practitioners disagree on terminology.

Public relations as a name was coined in the States at the beginning of the century. It was essentially concerned with how the company was seen by its customers and the public at large. Over the years this term has been widened to claim a concern with all the 'publics' of a company including customers, employees, investors and so on.

One of the several 'official' versions is that of the Institute of Public Relations (IPR) which defines public relations as 'the deliberate, planned, and sustained effort to establish mutual understanding between an organisation and its publics.'

A definition I find more helpful is given by Adele Biss of the Biss Lancaster consultancy, who says, public relations has the 'clearly defined purpose to influence the people who are most able to influence the success of your business or operation.'

Another problem of definition is that the general public (and many managers) continue to think of public relations as a propaganda exercise or the spreading of a few white lies. This impression is not helped by national newspaper and television journalists who consistently term any face-saving international episode as 'just another public relations exercise'.

Within the public relations industry much good work is being done by the national organisations in the UK – the IPR and the Public Relations Consultants Association (PRCA) – and in the US by the Public Relations Society of America (PRSA), in both educating their members to higher standards of professional skill and telling the world at large what PR is actually about. However, all this takes time and there is no quick or easy way to break down a detrimental image built up over years and reinforced daily by unsympathetic commentators.

PRESS RELATIONS

This is another PR (as are Proportional Representation, Puerto Rico and Populus Romanus. Confusing, isn't it!) This PR is merely *one* aspect of public relations itself: that of making regular and sustained contact with members of the Press – newspapers and magazines, radio and television. A press relations officer (PRO for short) does just that and works inside a company or organisation, usually at a junior level to the public relations manager.

Some company managers have the mistaken impression that public relations itself is simply and solely press relations, (an impression also given by some PR agencies). However, most communication professionals have long realised that sending out press releases and collecting column inches of the published stories is only one (and often a minor) part of an effective and efficient corporate communication exercise.

PR SPECIALISTS

Public relations consultancies have further compounded the confusion by specialising in certain areas of communication activity such as City, investor relations, industrial relations, parliamentary, crisis communication, employee communication, business to business and high tech.

Such specialising has encouraged some consultancies to stress that they possess a 'one-stop' or 'full service' agency. Trading rather like a communication supermarket, they claim to offer the customer a width of choice to save them having to pick one specialist (say, a parliamentary lobbyist) from Blink Limited and another (say, an investor relations advisor) from Blank & Associates.

In reaction to this growth of large, multi-purpose agencies, many of the smaller consultancies are now claiming that, because of their size, they can offer a more personal and effective service.

PUBLIC AFFAIRS or CORPORATE AFFAIRS

This is a title usually taken by an in-company director who wishes to sound a cut above the Public Relations Manager. In general, the work involved tends towards the City and government and investor relations – but, again, there is no standardisation.

ORGANISATIONAL COMMUNICATION

This is a more awkward variant of corporate communication but has a following in North America as well as the phrase 'business communication', and both are being used increasingly due to the work of the influential International Association of Business Communicators (IABC).

PUBLICITY

This is a hangover from the time when the publicity officer or publicity manager was responsible for the company's public face and handled advertising, exhibition stands, packaging, brochures and often a small design studio. Such titles still exist but it's a confusing anachronism which falls between the three stools of advertising, marketing and public relations.

ADVERTISING

One could imagine that this activity, at least, is straight-forward. It's the business of presenting the company's selected messages to one or more audiences through advertisements: slogans on posters, copy in publications, words and music on television and radio and film. It's handled by advertising agencies who, like the public relations consultants, often tend to specialise in one or more areas such as financial, business to business or recruitment. A 'full service' agency will plan your advertising, create the advertisements, select and buy the media, produce the advertisements and evaluate the campaign.

In addition, a growing number of agencies are buying or merging with other communication companies specialising in design, press relations, public relations, recruitment, typesetting or printing. The value of such communication conglomerates has yet to be proved but the trend is producing a growing stream of mergers from both sides of the public relations/advertising fence. It's good that PR and advertising are now beginning to work together within the corporate communication field but are they possibly getting too close for comfort?

MARKETING

This would seem to have little to do with our subject. It is, as the Institute of Marketing reminds us, 'the management process responsible for identifying, anticipating and satisfying consumer requirements profitably'. But such a broad definition often means that it is the marketing director who controls a large part of the communication process in a company, adding to traditional areas of sales planning and support, the adjacent fields of advertising and press and consumer relations as well as more distant regions such as employee publications. There are also independent consultants and agencies who see *all* communication exercises coming within the marketing umbrella.

MANAGEMENT CONSULTANTS

These agencies specialise in advising on the broad structure and direction that a company should take but this will inevitably involve some aspects of communication policy and activity. Indeed, many of the larger management consultancies have their own specialist departments dealing with such things as employee benefit communication, graduate recruitment, financial reporting and attitude surveys.

INDUSTRIAL EDITORS

Here is another traditional name which now means more than it says. These are a small but influential group of specialists who began by editing house journals and have now, under the banner of the British Association of Industrial Editors (BAIE), spread their wings to cover many other aspects of company communication including financial reporting and in-house video as well as every kind of publication from newsletters to company reports.

INVESTOR RELATIONS

This is a relatively new activity for British companies but investor relations managers have been going strong in the States since the 1960s. Concerned entirely with the City, with brokers' analysts and with large and small investors, they are the in-house equivalent of the public relations consultancies' City specialists. They, too, have their own association, the Investor Relations Society, and a growing involvement in financial reporting, both to shareholders and employees.

CORPORATE COMMUNICATION

Lastly, let me repeat from the first chapter of the book, my view that corporate communication is none and yet all of these activities and specialists. It is

THE TOTAL COMMUNICATION ACTIVITY GENERATED BY A COMPANY TO ACHIEVE ITS PLANNED OBJECTIVES

It is the company communicating to whichever audiences and with whatever media it cares to choose, *providing* it is aiming to achieve selected and planned objectives.

Advertising and public relations and investor relations and corporate design are thus all *part* of corporate communication – and not the other way round! This may be an unconventional approach but it makes sense. And, more importantly, it brings corporate communication out of this plethora of descriptions of consultancy jargon and plants it firmly within the daily working experience of every company manager.

Incidentally, note that it is corporate communication – without a final 's'. Tired of being called on to fix the company switchboard, recommend an answering machine or meet a computer salesman, I long ago adopted this form as being more accurate and left communications to the telecommunications specialists. It's a small point but another attempt to bring clarity out of confusion.

146

So much for nomenclature. If you're as puzzled by the diversity now as when you started this chapter, don't worry. By first light tomorrow another group of specialists will be jumping on the communication bandwagon (the accountants and the personnel managers are already well to the fore). In the final analysis it doesn't really matter *what* all these people call themselves. It would be helpful if they all complied with some British Standards description but communication is never that simple. Providing you now have a general appreciation of the specialist areas, don't worry overmuch about titles. They are of limited importance. What *is* important, as Edward Bernays implied, is not what these people are called but what they can actually do.

I've been everywhere, man!

Confronted with the task of entrusting all or part of the company's communication operation to an agency or an individual, most managers have the difficulty of knowing whether the people facing them across the desktop or grinning up in small, posed groups from the pages of a brochure, can actually do the job.

One slight disadvantage is that most in-company careers are built on accepted patterns of apprenticeship training and professional status through study and examination which is then nationally acknowledged as the acceptable standard for engineer, accountant or economist. The specialist areas now under review have no such definitive qualification foundations. True, there are many in the communication business who have letters after their names, indicating examinations passed in advertising, marketing, journalism, industrial editing and business communicating. There will be MAs, BAs, some PhDs and even the occasional MBA, although not until 1988 will the first MBAs with specialism in public relations be awarded from Cranfield. In academic qualifications in communication skills the UK lags far behind North America.

If you are faced with a CAM Dip or an FIPR, MAIE or ABC then that is a bonus but there are still many competent corporate communicators in the UK who have passed no examinations so may I suggest that your basis for selection should lie in a three-decker sandwich of:

▷ **EXPERIENCE/QUALIFICATION**
▷ **RECOMMENDATION**
▷ **COMPATIBILITY**

Showered with certificates

Experience is often won hard and early in the communication world by going in as personal assistant, secretary, office junior or trainee, picking up the essential facts and working jargon, and emerging three or four years later as an aspiring young executive. However, experience is *not* as speedily gained as some advertisements in the trade press would have us believe. So although the majority of communicators will be younger than you might expect, don't confuse enthusiastic brashness with knowledgeable competence.

Evidence of previous work will be most important in selecting your specialists because that, too, is all part of the experience. Public relations and advertising agencies will often stage an hour's presentation with slide or video show and printed material to illustrate selected case histories. Those dealing with the printed word will have no difficulty in giving a flavour of their best work. Photographers and designers will produce their portfolios and video and film companies a showreel of examples. It is less easy for the management consultant or market researcher to provide concrete reassurances but they too will be able to provide a selection of case histories.

Be circumspect when faced with such evidence. Very few communicators knowingly try to pull the wool over prospective clients' eyes but it can happen. An advertising or public relations campaign can be presented as the entire work of one team when in fact they were responsible for only one part of it; an editor's name can appear on the cover of a company publication when the majority of the work was done by an outside agency; a photograph may be brilliant because the photographer was coached by a brilliant director. On the whole, everything will be what your professional communicators say it is – but just be careful.

And please *don't* pay any attention to those who produce details of prizes and awards won as reasons why you should hire them. The professional communicating competitions – and there are many, from videos to PR campaigns, from company newspapers to annual reports – are very worthwhile *up to a point*. They are valuable to those who enter and to the industry as a whole for example and inspiration. But these people know the background to the competition: the restrictions, the number of entries, the standard reached, the calibre of the judging. You don't, and you'll find it safer to leave the list of certificates, medals and trophies *out* of your reckoning.

Tell me about whatsisname

Recommendation from other companies will be one of your most helpful signposts in making a communication appointment. If you are thinking of using a particular agency then the names of their current clients can be found in the annual trade directories. Individual consultants and smaller agencies should also be willing to give you a list of clients – and make sure they're *current*, say within the last two years. A phone call to your opposite number in a handful of client companies will at least give you a feel for the person or people you're considering.

If you simply want a list of names to start with, this comes direct from the professional association concerned. A somewhat more ambitious service is provided in the advertising industry where one publication and two video services provide a printed or visual synopsis of a range of agencies. A similar video service gives a selection of PR agencies.

Remember that one difference between hiring communicators for the company as opposed to many other professionals is that

YOU HAVE TO WORK WITH THEM

Earlier on I recalled the company man who asked 'Still

communicating like mad?' He'd forgotten that it wasn't just me, the specialist, who had to communicate: it was, had to be, a *joint* effort. Everything we've been saying so far points to that fact. So, whoever you finally choose, you have to be able to work with them, you have to be able to get on, they have to be *compatible*.

And that is the string by which many of the smaller agencies and independent consultants will try to pull in your business. They will claim that if you use a large group you will be initially impressed by the formidable phalanx of the big boys from the boardroom but when it gets down to day-to-day working you will be left to the untender mercies of a second year assistant you've never seen before.

Taking a broad view, that's unfair: you are just as liable to have a body change in a small group as in a large; but it *is* a possibility, so make sure that before you sign a contract with an outside company you meet and talk with the people who are *actually going to handle your account*. They're the ones who matter.

What about the green stuff?

'But excuse me.'

'Yes, Clarence?'

'Er – choosing a communicator, someone to handle the media ...'

'Yes.'

'Well, you've talked about experience, and examples of work, and personal recommendation and, er, what else?'

'Compatibility?'

'Oh yes, compatibility. But you haven't said anything about, er ...'

'What?'

(*Sotto voce*) 'Money'.

'Oh, that. Yes, well it's about time it was mentioned. Let's see ...'

The trouble with money is that it often takes too high a place in the corporate communicating programme. Advertising campaigns are too often described by what they cost. ASDA BILLS £1.5m WITH XYQ&Z reads the typical headline.

The growth of nationalised industry flotations is now driving public relations campaigns into similar news headlines. The 'top' PR and advertising agencies in the country are increasingly rated not by the quality of their work but by their annual client fees. Far too many decisions to employ a particular printer, artist, photographer, writer, PR consultancy, ad agency or market research company are decided on the lowest possible quotation as if *all* printers, artists, photographers etc were able to produce work to the same standard but at different prices.

Certainly there has to be a place for planned budgeting and cost efficiency in the corporate communication programme, but *please* don't give undue attention to the figures at the end of the column. Ask, rather, what you're getting for your money in terms of quality, experience, professional skill, compatibility and ideas. If what you are getting is achieving – or looks like being able to achieve – your communication objectives in the way you want, then cost may have to take a lower place in your list of priorities.

Having reached the question of price let me suggest one or

two pointers to help you deal with hiring and paying the communicating pipers.

Talking about money

▷ There is no standard method of paying for work by outside agencies and consultants but most of the professional associations will provide a guide to current practice.

▷ Usually you will need to sign a contract for *permanent* work (such as regular servicing and advice on communication matters) and agree a quotation for *one-off* projects such as a video film or an annual report.

▷ This will be as a result of some kind of presentation outlining how the work is to be done. Sometimes, as for a complete advertising or PR campaign, this will be elaborate and detailed and will entail the company making the 'pitch': considerable expense in both time and materials. Once again there are no rules, but you should be prepared to pay a nominal sum for such a presentation. Such a suggestion was once anathema but the times are changing.

Don't, as a matter of policy, ask for too many quotations. Unless you are putting an assignment out to open tender, three will usually be quite sufficient.

▷ Payment may be arranged in various ways for a long-term service agreement but the usual method is a fixed sum monthly or quarterly in advance, irrespective of how much work is done, and a payment in arrears covering all incidental expenses. Other agencies work on an hourly or daily rate, charging you for exactly how much time your work has taken and who was involved – more for an account director, less for a copy writer or research interviewer.

Advertising agencies work in a slightly different way: reaping much of their fee from the commission they receive from the media in which you advertise.

▷ Some consultants and agencies will charge a service fee for all the invoices passing through their hands – photography, design, printing – as a straight percentage cut, often 15 per cent of the bill plus commission total. Some don't. Make sure you know which method is in use as small percentages of large printing bills can add an unacceptable bulge at the end of your budget.

▷ Many independents in the communication business are small with limited cash reserves. They depend, like all small businesses, on quick payment of their invoices, particularly when they have already paid out money on your behalf for other media services. Make sure your company understands that basic financial need and meets it. No one enjoys chasing unpaid bills.

▷ **If you have a communication specialist working _inside_ the company you'll need to get an idea of current levels of pay. Again, the professional associations are the people to contact. They all monitor membership profiles through regular surveys.**

In or out?

By careful selection you will be able to find specialists to handle every type of medium, to evaluate your audiences and select and prepare the messages to be communicated.

But should these people work inside or outside the organisation?

Norman Hart, former Director of the CAM Foundation, says:

> '*There is no reason why a company shouldn't handle its own advertising. Indeed, this used to be the case when agencies were no more than agents acting on behalf of publishers. Recent research, however, shows that the vast majority of advertising by companies is planned, placed and executed by agencies. And there are good reasons for this over and above the very obvious need to keep one's own staff at a minimum level consistent with efficient business operation.*'

His reasons include a wide variety of expertise, group creativity, media buying power, independent advice and high quality. And, in general, those comments can be applied to any other major communication activity from employee communication through public relations to investor relations.

At the beginning of 1987 the electronics giant Plessey decided to transfer its large public relations account from the Charles Barker Lyons agency into its own keeping. There was no disagreement; it was a perfectly amicable arrangement, but why was it necessary? As company PR Director Peter Baillie recalled in *PR Week*:

> *'I came to Plessey from a company that handled all its public relations activity itself. I was surprised to find that Plessey entrusted everything to an outside consultancy.'*

But for another view turn to the British glassmakers Pilkington. In 1986 its Group Communications Adviser, David Wood, told *PR Week*:

> *'A great many of the smaller operating divisions ... employ consultancies, but we prefer to handle the bulk of the corporate public relations from here at head office ... Of course, there is a danger that we could become too inward looking, and I suppose that is where a consultancy comes in, providing a more detached perspective.'*

These reactions suggest that the wholesale acceptance of an All Our Own Work in-house communication policy makes as little sense as entrusting the whole communication programme to outside consultants.

The point is this: whoever has management responsibility for the communication process has to enjoy the freedom to bring into play the right combination of in- and out-of-house skills and resources to accomplish the task – within budget, of course.

All companies have differing communication needs but, just as we have seen that it's essential for the audiences, the messages and the media to be evaluated and selected, so we need to turn the same critical eye on who is to be used to control the media on our behalf, whether from inside or outside the company.

In summary, an internal department, headed by a corporate communication director reporting directly to the Top Man, whether chairman, chief executive or managing director, is essential for the achievement of the company's planned corporate communication programme. In addition, there should be full support from the outside specialists we have mentioned, on both short-term and long-term contracts, selected depending on the company's current strategies.

How those strategies can be researched, operated and achieved is the theme of our final chapter.

11
Winning through

Beware window dressing

THE COMPANY SECRETARY (and potential Board member) was sent on a three-month residential course at a prominent business school. On his return, bubbling with excitement and bursting with new ideas, he was interviewed by the Chairman.

'These courses are all very well,' said the great man, 'and I'm sure you've learnt plenty of new techniques but ...'

'I have indeed!' enthused the Company Secretary. 'Cash flow systems, management appraisal programmes, corporate communication strategies ...'

'Splendid, splendid', said the Chairman. 'Just don't imagine you're going to be allowed to change anything round here!'

☆　☆　☆

SO OFTEN seminars, training courses and books which encourage managers to reconsider traditional views and implement change are attended, watched and read – but not acted upon. They become nothing more than the superficial window dressing of the company showroom; fine in theory but never put to practical use.

Since we entered the corporate communication wood we have discussed the role which management must play in the communication process, appraised the company audiences, evaluated the messages, reviewed the available media and met the specialists. We have seen how audiences, messages and media can be brought together, in a number of company case histories.

But we can only penetrate halfway into the wood – from then on we are on our way out! There is a limit to the number of seminars we can attend, the videos we can watch, the magazines and books we can read. The time comes when we must do something about it; when theory must give way to practice.

Look on this survey – and on this

Resolved to take the final step into active communication but faced with an apparently limitless selection of audiences, messages and media, managers often need a finite starting point, an acceptable focus for discussion and decision. That focus has already been mentioned; it is the foundation of the corporate communication pyramid – research.

Quantitative and qualitative research is essential for the effective corporate communication programme, for without facts we cannot begin to work out the necessary strategy. We may have seen the light at the end of the wood but so many questions remain unanswered:

▷ **What exactly should we try to communicate?**
▷ **What do our audiences already think of us?**
▷ **Where do we need to concentrate our activities?**
▷ **What are the best methods to use in our particular industry?**
▷ **What, for heaven's sake, *are* our objectives?**

We need a benchmark – some hard facts and figures, around

which to talk and plan and activate and this basic information will come from researching our choice of audience.

We may decide to check on the company's current reputation among investors, bankers and stockbrokers, in which case the use of a City panel or a series of face-to-face interviews may be needed.

Our employees' views may need to be gathered by a communication audit (a snapshot of the company seen through their eyes) or a full-scale attitude survey.

We may want to look at how our dealers, customers or the general public see the company and its services or products, an operation which can be carried out by phone, on the street, in the home or through the post.

And if we are committing ourselves to a total corporate communication strategy, we will need to commission a number of such surveys in all these areas – attitude surveys, communication audits, awareness surveys, readership surveys – and repeat them at monthly, yearly or two-yearly intervals.

But in identifying such a starting point haven't we already stuck up too many flagpoles? It is often prudent and eye-opening to start the survey process itself by arranging in-depth interviews with every company director and senior executive to see how far *they* agree on the present state of the company and its future course. How do *they* view the need for corporate communication?

Market research – or audience research if that links the name closer to the subject in hand and away from political parties and washing powder – is skilled and specialised work. As with the other communication specialists, there is no shortage of research consultancies. The Market Research Society and its yearbook will supply names and addresses and, again, personal recommendations from other companies will be valuable in helping you decide which consultancies to approach and employ.

The rest is strategy

Once the essential information has been gathered, the next stage of the strategy – what objectives are to be achieved, with what and how – can be built into place by the corporate communication team and its external specialists. As the communication programme begins to operate so further regular research will be needed to monitor its progress and, at appropriate points, evaluate results, so that the programme becomes a valuable, constructive part of corporate life, not half a dozen platitudes in the company's annual report.

The corporate communication programme must not be allowed to slip away from the working environment of the company into the corporate shop window to gather dust. The subjects of the past ten chapters – audiences and messages and media – are too important to be relegated to a lower place on the management agenda. As we said on the first page, communication is the way in which the company makes and keeps contact with those who affect its life and growth.

CORPORATE COMMUNICATION IS OF STRATEGIC IMPORTANCE

When Don Craib, Chairman of Allstate Insurance, received the top management award given by the International Association of Business Communicators, he summed up the principles of corporate communication as he saw it from the top of a successful company which had worked hard to tailor its communication strategy to the current needs of the business environment.

He said that his company's experience was an example of two fundamental principles that are gaining widespread acceptance within the corporate world.

'First, communication strategy must be developed in the same way that business strategy is developed. It must be orientated to specific objectives. The results must be measured, and the plan modified if it is not meeting its goals.

'And secondly, communication strategy must be developed in concert with the business strategy. If it's not, it's a waste of time and money. If communication is made a full partner in the strategic planning process, it can help a company bridge the critical gap between intent and execution.'

Whether we head a department, a division or the company itself, those two statements make good sense. We need to establish a communication programme which is not rooted in the personality of the Top Man or in management factions or fashions, but in the on-going business strategy of the company, running in concert with it and being given the same level of commitment.

But, more than this, we need to convince ourselves that corporate communication is not some nebulous, intangible theory confined to textbook paragraphs and seminar schedules. It is grounded in the individual will and purpose of every manager in the company, which means that its power and effectiveness is not *primarily* a question of fine words, more money, snappier advertising or slicker brochures, but informed and committed *people* working towards common objectives.

Corporate communication works – if only we will let it. Making it work is up to you!